THOMAS COOK
Travellers

MADEIRA

BY
CHRISTOPHER CATLING

AA

Produced by AA Publishing

Written by Christopher Catling

Original photography by Jon Wyand

Edited, designed and produced by AA Publishing.
© The Automobile Association 1995.
Maps © The Automobile Association 1995.

Distributed in the United Kingdom by AA Publishing,
Norfolk House, Priestley Road, Basingstoke,
Hampshire RG24 9NY.

A CIP catalogue record for this book is available from the
British Library.

ISBN 0 7495 0949 X

Reprinted 1996

Published by AA Publishing (a trading name of Automobile Association
Developments Limited, whose registered office is Norfolk House,
Priestley Road, Basingstoke, Hampshire RG24 9NY. Registered number
1878835) and the Thomas Cook Group Ltd.

Colour separation: BTB Colour Reproduction, Whitchurch, Hampshire.

Printed by: Edicoes ASA, Oporto, Portugal.

Cover picture: *Câmara de Lobos*
Title page: *the grandeur of the Madeiran landscape*
Above: *the friendliness of the people*

Contents

About this Book

	BACKGROUND
	FIRST STEPS
	WHAT TO SEE
	GETTING AWAY FROM IT ALL
	DIRECTORY

This book is divided into five sections, identified by the above colour coding.

Background gives an introduction to the island – its history, geography, politics and culture.

First Steps offers practical advice on arriving and getting around.

What to See is an alphabetical listing of places to visit, interspersed with walks and drives.

Getting Away From it All highlights places off the beaten track where it is possible to relax and enjoy peace and quiet.

Finally, the **Directory** provides practical information – from shopping and entertainment to children and sport, including a section on business matters. Special highly illustrated **features** on specific aspects of the island appear throughout the book.

Fishing boats at São Tiago Fortress, Funchal Old Town

BACKGROUND

*I should think the situation
of Madeira the most
enviable on the whole earth.
It ensures almost every
European comfort together
with almost every
tropical luxury.*

H N COLERIDGE,
*Six Months in the West Indies,
in 1825.*

Introduction

*M*adeira is a fascinating blend of contrasting and unlikely ingredients, a place that reminds you of other far-flung destinations, while remaining uniquely itself.

mountaintops where you can enjoy a rare sense of stillness and peace as you admire the magnificent panoramas.

Exploring these lofty and silent peaks it is easy to forget that bustling Funchal is just two hours' drive away. Funchal is also part of Madeira's rich texture and it is a pleasure to return to the capital at

The steep terraced hillsides with their burgeoning banana crops may put you in mind of Bali or the Philippines: English roses and perennials grow in profusion alongside Asian orchids and Indian tulip trees; the island's fragrant eucalyptus woods recall Australia while the gorse-covered moorlands of the central plateau could be in the Scottish Highlands. The architecture of Madeira's capital evokes yet another place and time – the elegant balconies and shaded patios of Funchal seem straight out of the half-real, half-imaginary world of an Isabel Allende or Gabriel García Márquez novel. On top of all this, Madeira encompasses spectacular ravines and waterfalls, ever-changing skies and seas, and the end of a long day's tour, knowing that you can look forward to all the modern comforts of a luxurious hotel and the prospect of an excellent dinner – with or without a glass or two of Madeira.

Nature's profusion is all the more enjoyable when accompanied by such civilised comforts, and that is why Madeira – blessed with both – is such a delightful and satisfying holiday destination.

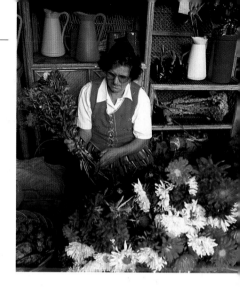

The island's abundant blooms are skilfully turned into beautiful bouquets

MADEIRA

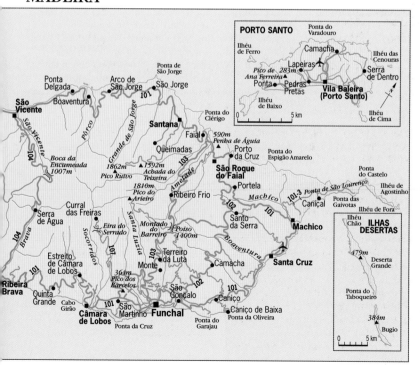

Geography

Madeira is a tiny island set in the Atlantic Ocean, a long way from anywhere. The nearest mainland is the coast of Morocco, 608km away. It is even further to Portugal, the country to which Madeira belongs, for the capital, Lisbon, is nearly 1,000km to the northeast.

Yet Madeira is not entirely alone: it is partnered by the smaller island of Porto Santo, 37km to the northeast, a popular summertime destination for Madeirans because of its long beach and golden sands. Another group of islands, the Ilhas Desertas, lie 16km to the southeast and are usually visible from Funchal; they live up to their name (Deserted Isles) by being uninhabited except for birds, seals and visiting naturalists. Much more distant, and also uninhabited, are the Ilhas Selvagens (Wild Islands) which lie 216km to the south; they also belong to the Madeiran archipelago, even though they are closer to the Spanish-owned Canary Islands than they are to Madeira.

The Terrain

Madeira is about the same size as Singapore, but beyond that all comparisons cease. You could drive the length of flat Singapore in under an hour, but the same journey would take up to half a day on mountainous Madeira. Distances are magnified by the steepness of the terrain. From the island's main east–west mountain range, numerous high ridges run north and south to the coast. All roads have to take a tortuous zigzagging route in order to negotiate the deep valleys and ravines that lie in between. This contorted terrain was very aptly described in a 19th-century guidebook which recounted a meeting between Christopher Columbus and Queen Isabella of Spain. The queen asked Columbus to describe Jamaica to her. He picked up a piece of paper, crumpled it between his hands and put it down again, saying 'This will give you a better idea of the island's appearance than any of my words'. Precisely the same will do for Madeira.

Another antiquated guidebook describes Madeira poetically as 'surrounded by an abysmal ocean'. The truth of this is brought home as you tour

Every inch of available land is farmed

The drama of Madeira's volcanic peaks is enhanced by the play of the elements

the island, especially the northern side where great Atlantic waves break against the high cliffs that line this coast. Sea and land meet abruptly on the island, with no gently shelving beaches in between – just a jumble of jagged rocks and grey pebbles. Below the waterline the cliffs continue for 1,000m or more before reaching the seabed.

Madeira's Economy

Surrounded by such a deep and dangerous element, the people of Madeira have tended to turn their backs upon the sea, and the island's tiny fishing fleets employ only a handful of hardy adventurers. Instead most Madeirans make their living from the hard graft of agriculture, tending the land by hand because there is no space on the narrow terraces for machinery. Sugar, known as 'white gold', made the early settlers rich until competition from New World plantations drove prices down. Today it is the yellow gold of bananas and the liquid gold of Madeira wine that sustains the island economy, along with tourism and handicrafts, including wickerwork and embroidery.

Madeira also benefits from funds from so-called 'emigrants' – islanders who have gone abroad to seek their fortune working in the Venezuelan oil industry, or in shops, restaurants and hotels in Britain, South Africa or Australia. The money they send home to help their families is a very significant element in the island's invisible economy and it explains why there are so many banks based in Funchal, competing against each other for the emigrants' accounts.

MADEIRA IN FIGURES
Population: 280,000 (of whom 86 per cent live on the sunny south of the island, including 100,000 in the capital, Funchal)
Area: 738 sq km
Length: 56km east to west
Width: 19km north to south
Highest point: Pico Ruivo (1,862m)
Sea depth: 6,000m in the Canary Basin, just 83km west of Madeira

History

20 million years ago
Volcanic eruptions begin beneath the
Atlantic, building up layers of lava which
finally rise above the surface of the sea to
create the Madeiran islands.

1.7 million years ago
The Madeiran volcanoes become extinct.
Seeds dropped by birds or washed up on
Madeira's shores thrive in the volcanic
soils and grow to form dense woodland
that cloaks the island.

2,000 years ago
The island of Madeira is known to
Phoenician, Roman and North African
sailors but is never colonised and has no
indigenous people.

1418
Prince Henry 'The Navigator' (son of
King João I of Portugal) sponsors several
voyages of discovery. One of these, led by
João Gonçalves Zarco, sets out to explore
the Guinea Coast of Africa. Blown off
course by violent storms Zarco finally
finds shelter off an island which he names
Porto Santo (Blessed Port) in gratitude.

1420
Zarco returns to investigate Porto Santo
further and discovers a much larger island
to the southwest; this he calls Ilha da
Madeira, the Island of Wood.

1425
After setting fire to the island's woods,
settlement begins in earnest. The island's
climate and fertile soil prove ideally
suited to the growth of sugar-cane and
early settlers grow rich producing 'white
gold'.

1452
The first slaves are brought from Africa
and the Canaries to build Madeira's
terraces, dig the irrigation channels and
work the fields.

1478
Christopher Columbus visits Madeira to
buy sugar. He later marries Filipa Moniz,
daughter of Bartolomeu Perestrello, the
first governor of Porto Santo.

1514
The island's first census reveals that
Madeira has 5,000 inhabitants.

1542
The defensive walls around Funchal,
built to protect the city from pirate
attacks, are completed.

1566
Despite the walls, 1,000 French pirates
attack Funchal, kill the governor and 250
Madeirans and loot the island's mansions
and churches in one of the worst raids in
Madeira's history.

1580
Philip II of Spain occupies Portugal and
Madeira comes under Spanish rule.

1614
Madeira's population has now risen to
28,345, of whom at least 3,000 are slaves.

1640
The Portuguese revolt against Spanish
rule and regain their independence under
King João IV.

1662
Catherine of Braganza, daughter of King
João IV, marries Charles II of England.
As part of the marriage settlement
commercial privileges are granted to
English merchants, who settle on
Madeira and increasingly come to
dominate the profitable Madeira wine
trade.

1775
Slavery is declared illegal in Portugal.

1803
600 are drowned when flash floods
inundate Funchal. The city's three rivers

are enclosed by high walls to prevent future disasters.

1807–1813
British troops are garrisoned on Madeira to prevent Napoleon invading the island. The strikingly blue eyes and fair hair of some Madeirans are the genetic legacy of this period.

1852
In the same year, cholera carries off 7,000 victims and the island's vineyards are devastated by mildew. New and more resistant vine varieties are planted and the cultivation of bananas is stepped up.

1887
The island's economy is boosted by the large number of European tourists visiting for the winter, or staying in Madeira *en route* to postings in South America and the Far East.

Prince Henry 'The Navigator'

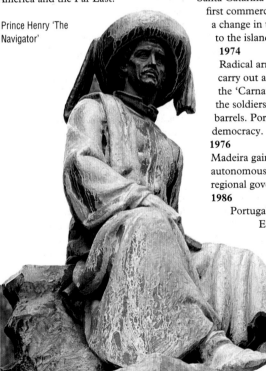

1891
The luxurious Reid's Hotel opens its doors to wealthy visitors.

1916–1917
German U-boats twice shell Funchal from the harbour, causing minor damage.

1931
Madeirans declare a general strike in protest against the regime of the Portuguese dictator, Salazar. Troops from Lisbon are used to put down the rebellion. From this time on, Madeirans begin emigrating in large numbers in search of a better life.

1949–1958
Flying-boat services operate between Southampton and Madeira.

1964
Santa Catarina airport opens and the first commercial flights begin, marking a change in the type of visitor coming to the island.

1974
Radical army officers in Lisbon carry out a bloodless coup known as the 'Carnation Revolution' because the soldiers carry flowers in their gun barrels. Portugal enters a new era of democracy.

1976
Madeira gains the status of an autonomous region, with its own regional government and president.

1986
Portugal's entry into the European Community gives Madeira access to development funds which are used to extend the airport runway, build new roads and improve the island's infrastructure.

Tales of Discovery

Many stories have been told about the discovery and colonisation of Madeira, and many myths persist to this day; one is that Madeira is the last vestige of the drowned continent of Atlantis; another is that the lost treasure of the notorious pirate, Captain Kidd, is buried on one of the Ilhas Selvagens.

The truth is more prosaic. It is known for a fact that the Madeiran islands were familiar to navigators long before Porto Santo and Madeira were officially 'discovered' by João Gonçalves Zarco in the year 1420.

Pliny, the 1st-century AD Roman writer, called them the 'Purple Islands' because of the distinctive colour of Madeira's volcanic rocks and soil. The Medici map of 1351, drawn by Genoese cartographers, was the first to depict Madeira and give it a name – Isola delle Lolegname (Island of Wood). The same name – Ilha da Madeira in Portuguese – was used by Zarco when he landed in 1420, laying claim to the island on behalf of Portugal.

The story of Robert Machin

Facts, though, are rarely as romantic as the tales embroidered by sailors with time on their hands as they sailed the Atlantic carrying cargoes of Madeiran sugar, grain and wine. About 100 years after Zarco's discovery, the chronicler Valentine Fernandes published a different account, which he no doubt heard in some harbourside bar. This concerns a Bristol merchant, Robert Machin, who was blown out into the Atlantic by a storm while sailing to Portugal. Ending up within sight of Madeira, Machin went ashore to investigate. His mutinous crew decided to abandon Machin, but they got caught up in another storm which drove them

on to the Moroccan coast where they were taken prisoner, destined to serve as galley slaves.

Determined to return to civilisation, Machin built himself a raft. He, too, fell prey to Moroccan pirates and ended up in the same prison as his former crew. Machin then furiously attacked one of his fellow sailors, meaning to kill him in revenge. Astonished by the ferocity of the fight, Machin's gaolers forced him to explain his actions and it was not long before the whole story of the mysterious island at the edge of the known world began to circulate. It was only a matter of time before Henry the Navigator heard the story and sent Zarco out to investigate.

Even more romantic versions of Machin's story circulated in the 17th century in which he is portrayed as an English aristocrat eloping with his sweetheart, Anna d'Arfet (or Anne of Hertford).

Shipwrecked on Madeira, she dies of exposure and he of a broken heart. Zarco is said to have found their graves when he stepped ashore in 1420, inspiring him to name the spot Machico, after Machin's name.

Another Madeiran legend has it that Zarco set fire to Madeira – this being the fastest way to clear the island's dense woodland – and that the forests blazed for seven years.

In fact, clearance was probably much more selective; the island's timber was a valuable resource, used for building houses, ships and the crates in which sugar and other crops were packed.

Columbus and Madeira

Another colourful and persistent story has it that Christopher Columbus lived

on both Madeira and Porto Santo for several years; here he married, fathered his only son and became convinced by the exotic plant remains washed up on Madeira's shores that sailing westward would bring him to the spice islands of the Indies. He therefore sailed back to Lisbon determined to raise funds for an expedition to test his theory. The story sounds too neat, too well honed to be true, and for many years the Madeirans themselves were among the most sceptical. Nowadays, however, it looks as if the legend may contain some truth, and that Columbus may have even returned to live on Madeira, off and on, after his discovery of the New World. For the 1992 quincentenary celebrations, Madeirans decided to acknowledge and capitalise on the Columbus connection for the first time, and visitors to Porto Santo (page 140) can now visit the Casa de Colombo (House of Columbus) museum with its portraits of the great man, and early maps of Madeira and the Americas.

Columbus (left) heads for the New World (below)

Politics

*T*he winds of political change came late to Madeira, which had to endure until 1968 the totalitarian regime of the Portuguese dictator, António d'Oliveira Salazar. Salazar's successor, the marginally more liberal Prime Minister Caetano, was then deposed in the Carnation Revolution of 1974, when the military took control but symbolised their desire for peaceful change by carrying flowers in their gun barrels.

Creating a new democracy

At the time of the 1974 revolution there were many in Madeira who wanted complete independence from Portugal. This reaction was understandable – under the long years of the Salazar regime Madeirans were made to feel as if they were helpless inhabitants of a remote little island who would be lost without mother Portugal. At the beginning of every day, Madeiran school children were made to repeat: *A nação é tudo; tudo pela nação* (the nation is all; all to the nation). This fine-sounding slogan was used to disguise an ugly truth: the Lisbon government had been milking the Madeiran economy for decades, appropriating revenues from exports and tourism, so that what should have been a prosperous island was left with some of the worst poverty and deprivation in Europe.

Politically active Madeirans were determined that islanders should in future be in charge of their own destiny; they were eventually persuaded that it might be better to remain part of Portugal, but as an autonomous region.

This means that Madeira now controls its own economy and sets its own taxes and customs duties as well as deciding how much should be spent on health, welfare and educational programmes. The island still looks to the Portuguese mainland for its foreign and defence policies, and the brightest Madeiran students still go to Portugal for their university education, but since 1974 there has been a growing sense of island identity; the people of Madeira are proud of their history and culture and now tend to think of themselves as Madeirans first and foremost, rather than as Portuguese.

The system of government

Madeira, Porto Santo and the other islands of the archipelago make up what Madeiran newspapers call the RAM (Região Autónoma da Madeira). This is governed by the 50-seat regional parliament, based in Funchal, which has the power to pass legislation and deal with all issues directly affecting the islands. In practice many of the day-to-day decisions are taken by the executive committee consisting of the president, the vice-president and six secretaries. The island also has a number of town councils responsible for more local issues, and, on a broader stage, Madeira elects five representatives from the regional parliament who sit as members of the Lisbon-based Portuguese parliament.

Parties and personalities

Madeira's head of state since 1976 has been Dr Alberto João Jardim, an extremely popular and charismatic figure whose picture appears almost daily on the front page of Madeiran newspapers as he cuts the ribbon to inaugurate a new school or health clinic. President Jardim's PSD (Popular Social Democrat) party holds most of the seats in the regional parliament and regularly polls 70 per cent of the vote in elections, which are held every four years.

Dissent, such as it is, centres around the PS (Socialist) party and the right-of-centre CDS. The smaller parties are better represented at town council level,

and it is here that a conflict of policies occasionally takes place. It is hard, though, for opposition parties to dent President Jardim's popularity because he has presided over nearly two decades of unprecedented growth, during which the living standards of most Madeirans has improved very substantially – most villages now have electricity, schools and a health clinic, as well as a road link to the capital, Funchal, all of which were just a politician's dream in the 1970s. Even so, Madeirans have begun to talk about what the future holds once Jardim retires. The next president will have to tackle a whole new set of issues. This time the problems will be less to do with poverty and low living standards, and more to do with the pollution, untrammelled development and abandonment of the land that is resulting from the island's rising levels of prosperity.

PSD election poster (left) and government offices (below) in Funchal

Culture

Madeira is an island in transition from third-world levels of poverty to first-world prosperity. The change, not yet complete, has nevertheless been so rapid that you can simultaneously glimpse scenes from Madeira's past and from its future as you tour the island.

Driving into the village of Santana, for example, you are quite likely to catch sight of what looks like a walking haystack – a peasant farmer invisible beneath the great stack of hay that she is carrying to feed her cow. She and her family may well live in a traditional thatched A-framed house and cook in the open air over a wood fire. She may wash herself and her clothes in a nearby *levada* (irrigation canal), and the family may survive on an income of less than £120 (US$168) a year. Her husband will work tiny terraced fields by hand and will think nothing of carrying the produce he grows in wicker baskets for very long distances along steep and winding mountain paths to be left by the roadside for the local co-operative to collect.

Roads and change

There are still villages and farms in the island that are two hours' arduous walk from the nearest road, which have no electricity or television and where some of the inhabitants have never travelled to see the island's capital, Funchal.

Even so, the number of Madeirans who live this traditional life – spending all their waking hours in laborious work without the benefit of modern technology – is diminishing rapidly. Road-building programmes, partly funded by European Union grants, have been a major catalyst for change. As new roads are driven further into the remotest parts of Madeira's interior, electricity follows, generated by wind turbines located on the island's northern cliffs, or by water turbines powered by the outflow from reservoirs. Roads mean that farmers can drive their crops to the agricultural co-operative or sell direct to hotels and restaurants. Many now travel to Funchal every Friday to sell their produce in the lively Mercado dos Lavradores (Workers' Market).

Once a village is linked into the island's road network, it is only a matter of time before land-hungry urbanites begin to arrive, looking for plots on which to build a weekend home – or emigrants returning from overseas with a nest egg looking for somewhere to build

Shouldering a bundle of firewood: traditional Madeiran life is arduous

Carrying produce to market the old way: a scene now rarely witnessed

a retirement home. To the despair of those who love the island's traditional architecture and natural beauty, it will not be long before the scenic village is surrounded by newly built villas and the green hillsides splattered with bright orange roof tiles and white walls. To complete the transformation, tourists begin arriving by coach or taxi, shops, restaurants and even hotels are opened to cater for them and the village benefits from a general increase in prosperity.

Town and country

It is difficult to predict what long-term effect these changes will have on the culture of Madeira, although Funchal offers some clues as to how the rest of the island may develop. The Catholic church, which is still a major force in the lives of rural Madeirans, has far less power in the capital – so much so that many parish churches in Funchal are locked and unused. Where religious processions to honour the Virgin or a patron saint draw crowds of devotees in the village, only events like the New Year festivities and the Madeira Wine Rally attract similar numbers in the city. Funchal people see themselves as sophisticated and cosmopolitan, intellectual and, where religion is concerned, at best agnostic. Yet loyalty to the family remains as strong as ever it was and the people of Funchal are every bit as hardworking and entrepreneurial as their country cousins. What is more, there is a strong sense of pride in those things that make Madeira special and unique – its wines, landscapes and architecture and even the traditional costumes and dances which are worn and performed for pleasure and not merely for the sake of the tourist revenue.

Climate

*M*adeira is blessed with an almost perfect climate – it is never intolerably hot and never too cold. In winter the island's southerly latitude and the warmth given off by the sea combine to ensure that temperatures do not often dip below a pleasant 18°C.

This makes Madeira a popular destination for anyone seeking an escape from the icy grip of northern European winters. In summer, the trade winds help to keep Madeira cool and clouds build up to screen the island from the hot midday sunshine so temperatures rarely exceed 24°C. This makes Madeira a popular destination for mainland Portuguese visitors along with anyone else fleeing the searing heat of continental summers (by contrast, Madeirans themselves, looking for some really hot sunshine for a change, go and roast themselves on neighbouring Porto Santo, which in summer is usually very hot and dry).

Despite the equable nature of Madeira's climate, there is also great variety: temperatures drop rapidly with altitude and chill winds can blow on the mountaintops even in summer; that is why the stallholders who sell sweaters on the top of Pico do Arieiro (1,818m) enjoy a brisk trade. In winter you can often enjoy the experience of playing snowballs on the mountaintops in the morning and sunbathing by the hotel pool in the afternoon.

Even more enthralling is to walk among the high peaks of Madeira in brilliant sunshine while below you, cottonwool clouds shroud the island; you will feel on top of the world, especially since you know that less fortunate souls down at sea level are probably sheltering from the rain. Rain can be guaranteed to freshen up every day – only in July and August is it likely to be dry. Fortunately, in Funchal, the rainfall tends to come in short bursts: after a clear start to the day, clouds caused by condensation build up to a peak around noon but then shed their watery load to leave the late afternoon and evening clear and sunny once again.

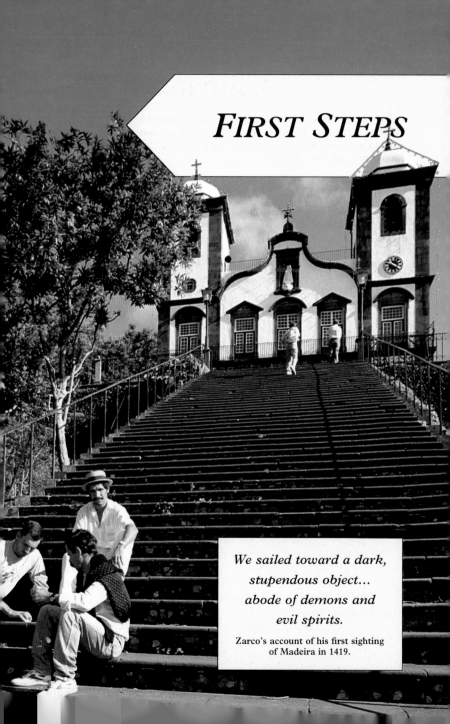

FIRST STEPS

We sailed toward a dark,
stupendous object…
abode of demons and
evil spirits.

Zarco's account of his first sighting
of Madeira in 1419.

INTRODUCTION

When Zarco first caught sight of Madeira in 1420 it was covered in cloud and he thought he was approaching the edge of the world – the place where, according to medieval cosmography, demons and evil spirits dwelled. By the time Zarco landed he had changed his view entirely and rapturously described the island as a place of 'lightsome beauty... the land of fairies'.

Today's traveller, arriving by air, still experiences a sense of journeying across endless ocean until the jewel-like island, intensely green and set in a crystal clear blue sea, suddenly appears on the horizon. All too quickly that vision is lost as you descend to Santa Catarina airport and are whisked off, with great efficiency, through the Funchal traffic to your hotel.

The first view on arrival: Madeira's Santa Catarina airport

Once you have settled into the hotel, it is easy to be seduced into spending all week by the poolside, strolling through the streets of Funchal or lingering for hours over lunch in some harbourside seafood restaurant. It is easy to forget that glimpse you had of the green mountains rising out of the sea – all too easy, in fact, to become part of that statistic that says 80 per cent of Madeira's visitors do not travel beyond the confines of Funchal. That would be a pity because the island's coastal and mountain landscapes are some of the most spectacular in Europe, and they are also very accessible by coach tour or taxi.

PLANNING YOUR TIME

The best strategy for enjoying the real Madeira is to spend the first day or so unwinding and getting to know Funchal, but then plan to take a tour on the second or third day of your stay. Too many people leave seeing the island until the last moment, signing up for a round-the-island tour towards the end of their visit, only to discover what pleasures they have been missing all week. Neither does it make sense to try and see all of Madeira in a day – a typical island tour involves travelling 150km, spending most of the day in a coach, and you will still only see a fraction of the island's varied charms. It is far better to begin by sampling the grandeur of the Madeiran countryside by means of a half-day tour – then you can decide how much more you want to see and do. For scenic value, the best short tours are those that take you to Curral das Freiras (also known as the Nuns' Refuge), to Pico do Arieiro, the island's third highest peak, to the trout farm at Ribeiro Frio and to Santana, with its traditional A-framed houses. Your hotel will have leaflets detailing all these tours, as will travel agents in Funchal, such as Blandys, at Avenida das Comunidades Madeirenses 1 (tel: 220162).

Despite initial impressions that all the tour operator's packages are the same, it is still worth shopping around. Not only do prices, timings and routes vary, some companies also offer excursions by eight-seater mini bus, which can be far more enjoyable than travelling as part of a bigger party on a coach. Remember, too, that the weather can often be clearer in the morning than in the afternoon, and while there is always a risk of clouds, mist or rain, the views can be better if you take a tour before lunch rather than after.

TRAVELLING INDEPENDENTLY

Many tour operators will also organise taxi excursions for you, which can be

Funchal's main seafront promenade, the Avenida do Mar

preferable to negotiating directly with the taxi drivers themselves. A good tour operator will find you a reliable taxi driver; that is, one who drives carefully (it is easy to suffer from travel sickness or vertigo on Madeira's steep and winding roads), one who knows the island thoroughly and one who speaks English (or any other language) fluently. Taxis can usually be hired by the half day (9am to 1pm or 1pm to 5pm) or for the full day, and though the rates are supposed to be fixed by the taxi drivers' association, most drivers try and charge more, so you should bargain them down. For two people sharing a taxi, the cost will be slightly greater than taking a coach tour, but for three or more sharing the cost, the taxi works out cheaper.

RIP-OFFS AND TOUTS

Madeira is remarkably free (as yet) of timeshare touts and similar nuisances but they do exist, and it is best to be forewarned. Timeshare touts are paid large sums of money to get you to sign an irrevocable and expensive contract, and they will use every tactic possible to get you to do so. These touts tend to hang around the Hotel Zone, so if you are pestered by them, return to your hotel at once and complain to the management.

You should also avoid unlicensed drivers offering tours or taxi services (some of whom double as timeshare touts). These people will charge you an extortionate rate and should be avoided in favour of yellow licensed taxis operating fixed or metered fares (see page 186). Most taxi drivers are thoroughly honest, but you should beware of taking their advice, especially when it comes to restaurants. They will tell you that they know somewhere really good, cheap and typically Madeiran; all too often this will be located out of town so that you pay a bigger taxi fare, and situated so far from any other restaurant that you have no choice but to eat there.

By the time you discover that it is also twice as expensive as downtown restaurants, the driver will have disappeared (though he will be back, in due course, to collect his commission from the restaurant owner). If you are aware of these tricks, they are easy to avoid, and you should have a carefree, enjoyable holiday.

THOMAS COOK'S
Madeira

The first reference to a Cook's holiday to Madeira is in 1885, when the island was included as part of a trip to the Portuguese mainland. In the early 20th century, steamers, which resembled 'floating hotels', departed regularly from London and Liverpool to make round-trip cruises to Madeira, calling at the Canary Islands as well. In the Traveller's Gazette, *in 1921, Madeira was described as 'this flower-bedecked isle under Ionian skies'.*

Official taxis in Funchal's main square

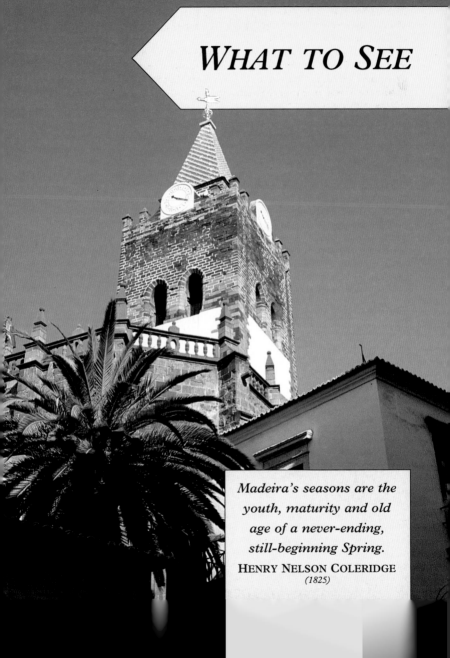

WHAT TO SEE

Madeira's seasons are the
youth, maturity and old
age of a never-ending,
still-beginning Spring.

HENRY NELSON COLERIDGE
(1825)

Funchal

*M*adeira's capital is an elegant city, once dubbed 'little Lisbon' by visiting mariners because of the grandeur of its cathedral and harbourside buildings. The city resembles a huge amphitheatre, sheltered by a semicircle of hills, with open views out across the harbour to the sea and the distant Ilhas Desertas.

FUNCHAL

Most of Madeira's hotels occupy elevated positions to the west of Funchal, built on the clifftops and hills to make the most of the views. From this Hotel Zone it takes upto 30 minutes to reach central Funchal on foot, or a few minutes by taxi. Madeirans themselves complain

The hills rise steeply above Funchal

about traffic and pollution in the capital, and the stench of diesel fumes can be oppressive during the morning and evening rush hours (around 9am and 5pm) but visitors from many other cities will consider Funchal delightfully quiet. It will be quieter still when the elevated expressway, currently under construction to the north of the city, takes through traffic out of the centre.

CITY OF FENNEL
The name Funchal comes from *funcho*, meaning fennel. Zarco gave this name to the spot where he landed in July 1420 because of the abundance of the sweet-smelling herb that he found in flower.

Central Funchal

Measures have already been taken to
route traffic out of the elegant avenues at
the very heart of the city. One of these is
Avenida Arriaga, lined with trees,
gardens, fountains, fashionable shops
and *belle époque* mansions, now the
prestigious premises of banks and
government departments (see Central
Funchal walk, page 62).

Traffic still uses the Avenida do Mar,
the city's wide seafront promenade, but
this is an ideal spot from which to admire
the short but colourful Madeiran sunset,
or for taking an after-dinner stroll (see
To the Waterfront walk, page 60). To
the right of the avenue is the busy
harbour area filled with container ships
and cruise liners. The existence of this
deep natural harbour was the reason why
Funchal developed as the island's capital,
rather than Machico, which once

rivalled Funchal in size and prosperity.
The great Molhe da Pontinha, the
breakwater which surrounds the harbour,
was built in 1895 and incorporates the
tiny fortified island of Loo Rock, midway
down its long concrete arm. More
fortifications survive to the landward side
of Avenida do Mar, including the Palácio
de São Lourenço. Bristling with cannons,
it was built in the 1520s to defend the
city against repeated piratical attacks and
later converted into the residence of the
island's 19th-century governors, one civil
and one military.

Following Avenida do Mar to its
easternmost limit you will reach the Zona
Velha, or Old Town (see The Old Town
walk, page 64), with its narrow cobbled
alleys and its outdoor restaurants serving
some of the best-value food to be had in
the capital. Between the Hotel Zone and
the Zona Velha lives the rest of the city
(see the Between the Rivers and Elegant
Mansions walks, pages 66 and 68
respectively), a wonderful jumble of
modern and old, where stylish shops
aimed at cruise passengers sit side by
side with antiquated general stores
selling daily necessities and smelling of
salt cod and dried herbs. The
architecture is equally varied and further
colour is added by the many flowersellers
and street traders who operate around
the cathedral and Mercado dos
Lavradores (Workers' Market), itself a
fascinating amalgam of sights and
sounds.

In short Funchal may be a small city,
but it is not to be underestimated – each
time you think you have covered every
inch of the ground you will turn a corner
and discover something entirely new.

Funchal's deep natural harbour, with the Hotel
Zone beyond

The Praça do Municipio (left) and decorated paving on Avenida Arriaga (below), Funchal

PAVEMENT PATTERNS

It pays to look down wherever you walk in Funchal to admire the style and craftsmanship of the humble pavements. In the Zona Velha, the streets are made from sea pebbles, rounded by the waves, carefully selected so that they are all of the same size, and set in mortar. The cobbles are hardwearing and quickly drain the water away when it rains.

Funchal's main square, the Praça do Município, is elegantly covered in a repeated series of fan shapes, alternately laid in dove-grey basalt and white marble. More flamboyant is Avenida Arriaga, with its heraldic flowers and fleurs-de-lis in black and white mosaic. In some parts of the city the paving is now sadly patched with asphalt where service trenches have been dug, but the art of making mosaic pavements is not dead: recently completed examples include the large Madeiran coat of arms in Praça de Cristovão Colombo south of the cathedral and the caravel, compass, sedan chair and wine-carrier with his yoke in Rua João Tavira, northwest of the cathedral.

Adegas de São Francisco

A visit to the Adegas de São Francisco (the St Francis Wine Lodge) is one of the most enjoyable ways that you can spend a couple of hours on Madeira, and if you are planning to take home a bottle or two of Madeira it is worth coming here first to learn about the history and production of this magnificent fortified wine.

The wine lodge is run by the Madeira Wine Company, a consortium whose shareholders include most of the famous names of the Madeira trade – names such as Blandy, Leacock and Luiz Gomes. Everything about the lodge has the appropriate patina of time and as soon as you enter you will be greeted by the delicious smell of old wood and wine. The timber buildings surround a cobbled courtyard overlooked by a wisteria-clad balcony. Some of the buildings date back

to the 16th century and were part of the island's Franciscan friary which closed in 1834 following the dissolution of all monastic orders operating in Portugal. Standing in various rooms around the lodge are huge barrels of mahogany and America oak; some 400,000 litres of precious wine are stored in this lodge alone, but this is a small fraction of the 1 million litres a year produced by the Madeira Wine Company alone and of the 4.5 million litres produced by the seven wine companies operating in the island. The sheer weight of these storage barrels means that the floors of the wine lodge have to be very strong – hence the massive timbers used as joists and supports, said to have come from ships either wrecked on Madeira or dismantled for salvage once they were no longer seaworthy.

Guided tours
If you join one of the excellent hour-long guided tours offered by the wine lodge you will first be shown an audio-visual presentation detailing the history of Madeira wine. Next you will visit the coopers' yard where you can watch wine barrels made of oak being repaired, cleaned or marked with branding irons. You will then be taken to see the warming rooms where Madeira wine is

Storage in oak barrels helps to impart flavour to Madeira wine heated in vast vats for six months using the natural warmth of the sun assisted by hot water pipes. Heating is essential to the character of Madeira wine, though its effects were discovered quite accidentally. The original Madeira, known as malmsey, was a pretty ordinary wine which sailors drank because it was cheap. Barrels of malmsey served the double duty of providing ballast and alcoholic stimulation on long sea journeys. Sailors then discovered that the wine improved when it was taken to the tropics, spending weeks or months in a hot hold. Now the wine does not leave Madeira until it has been bottled, but until the end of the 19th century it was still sent on board ship to the equator and back as an essential part of the production process. The other key ingredient is brandy, added to stop the

fermentation and fortify the wine, after which the slow process of maturation begins. As the tour reaches its conclusion you will be taken round a small museum full of leather-bound ledgers, ancient wine presses and old tools before returning to the downstairs wine bar, its walls frescoed with wine-harvest scenes, for a free tasting. After a glass or two of delicious wine you may be tempted to make a purchase, but don't get carried away – some of the rare bottles on offer cost over 50,000 _escudos!_

Avenida Arriaga 28 (tel: 742121). Open: Monday to Friday, 9am–1pm and 2.30–6pm; Saturday, 9am–1pm. Guided tours: Monday to Friday at 10.30am and 3.30pm; Saturday 11am. Admission charge for the guided tours.

Museum piece: an ancient wooden wine press

MADEIRA WINE

There are four basic types of Madeira, each named after the grape variety from which they are principally made. *Sercial* is an amber-coloured dry wine, often served as an aperitif or with soup or fish. It is made from grapes grown at around 800m; grapes grown at lower levels increase in sweetness because more of their sugars are concentrated by the sun. Thus *verdelho*, grown at around 500m, is a medium dry tawny-coloured wine for drinking with the main course. The nutty rich *bual* goes well with Stilton or chocolate and the sweetest Madeira is the rich, dark mellow *malmsey*, good with after-dinner coffee.

The gradual heating and cooling of the wine and the fortification with cane spirit (a type of brandy) gives Madeira its extraordinary longevity. A reserve wine will already be 5 to 20 years old and vintage Madeira must have spent 20 years in the cask and two in the bottle, but these are relative youngsters.

dinner held at Reid's Hotel in 1950, the British community in Madeira presented Churchill with a bottle that had previously been given to Napoleon when he anchored off the island on the way to exile in St Helena. The bottle was never drunk and came back to Madeira. Opening it and sharing it with his fellow guests, Churchill was not so much impressed by the Napoleon connection as by the thought that 'this wine was made when Marie Antoinette was still alive!'

History is imbibed when you sip Madeira, taking in aromas that – in some cases – have taken many decades to mature

The oldest surviving bottle dates to 1772 – when the cork was last replaced in 1991 the wine inside was analysed and found to be perfect. You can find wines for sale on Madeira at around 600,000 *escudos* that were bottled in 1863, while the American Civil War was still in progress.

Winston Churchill, a regular visitor to Madeira, was fond of the island's noble wines and pointed out that history was being sipped with every glass. At a

ALFÂNDEGA VELHA

The Alfândega Velha (Old Customs House) is one of Madeira's most ancient buildings, begun around 1477. In the 1970s it was converted to form the home of Madeira's regional parliament. For this reason it is only open to the public on rare occasions (if it is open, do go in to see the fine wood-carved ceiling) but you can walk round the exterior to look at the Manueline-style decoration of the stone-carved portals. The harbourside façade is now hidden by the modern circular debating chamber clad in white marble and widely held to be a blot on the face of an otherwise dignified building.

Rua da Alfândega. Not normally open.

CONVENTO DE SANTA CLARA

The Convent of the Order of Poor Clares was founded in the 15th century by two grand-daughters of the island's discoverer, João Gonçalves Zarco. Zarco himself, having lived to the ripe age of 80, was buried beneath the high altar of the conventual church. His simple tomb slab is not visible but there is an imposing 15th-century tomb at the rear of this church, often mistaken for Zarco's; in reality it belongs to his son-in-law, Martin Mendes Vasconcelos. Much of the rest of the church was rebuilt in the 17th century and the walls are lined from floor to ceiling with a carpet-like tapestry of yellow, white and blue *azulejos* tiles, making a rich geometric pattern. The timbered ceiling features a painted ship in full sail as well as floral and heraldic motifs. The heavy iron grille at the back of the church has an interesting story. Behind it is a stout wooden door which would be opened so that visitors could have limited communication with the nuns who lived

in the convent beyond. It is a reminder of the very isolated and withdrawn lives led by the nuns who were never allowed to leave their cloistered confinement – though the nuns of this convent did once flee their home – in 1566 – to escape a piratical attack, journeying inland to the hidden valley now named Curral das Freiras (Nuns' Refuge) in their honour (see page 86).

The tragic story of Maria Clementina

Many of the nuns were condemned to a life within convent walls by pious or penurious parents. The case of one nun became a *cause célèbre* in the 19th century and many foreign visitors to Funchal used to come to the convent to visit her, providing what little companionship and comfort was possible talking through a metal grille.

Maria Clementina was widely held to be the most beautiful girl on Madeira but her parents forced her to take the veil on her 18th birthday because they were unable to afford the dowry without which aristocratic young ladies found it hard to find a husband of similar rank. (Placing your daughter in a nunnery was also supposed to confer spiritual benefits on parents and child alike.) A year later, the newly established liberal government in Lisbon ordered the religious houses of Portugal to liberate any of their inmates who had been forced into taking monastic vows and who wished to leave. Maria was released and fell passionately in love with a handsome army officer. Before they could marry, however, Portugal's absolutist monarch dissolved the parliament and revoked all its laws. Maria was forced to return to the convent where she spent the rest of her life.

Abuses such as this eventually led the Portuguese parliament to dissolve all religious establishments, though today the Poor Clares have returned to Santa Clara, where they run a highly regarded school, part of which you will see if you wander through the convent to find the lovely peaceful 15th-century cloister, planted with citrus trees, which lies to the south of the church.

Calçada de Santa Clara. Open: daily, 9am–noon and 3pm–6pm except during church services. If the church door is closed, ring the bell at the convent entrance, to the right of the church, for admission.

Santa Clara's tranquil convent cloister, built soon after the island's discovery

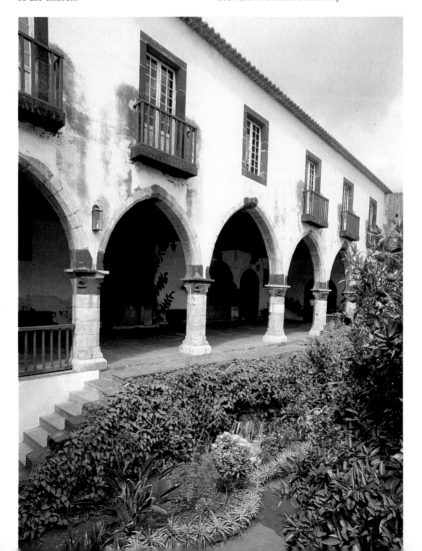

FOREIGNERS & MADEIRA

Madeira had no indigenous population when Zarco landed in 1420, but the island soon attracted adventurers of all nations – Flemish, Italian, Spanish, French and English. Many came as merchants who invested in land and made fortunes from sugar cultivation and the wine trade. English involvement in the island increased substantially after Charles II married Catherine of Braganza, daughter of King João IV of Portugal, in 1662. England very nearly gained Madeira as part of Catherine's dowry; it is said that the scribe who drew up the marriage contract was Madeiran and that patriotism led him to omit the island. English traders moved in anyway when Charles II passed a law in 1665 prohibiting the export of European goods to the English colonies in America, unless they were shipped through English ports in English ships.

Madeira was explicity excluded from this restriction and one result was the rapid growth of wine shipments from the island to the colonies. The Americans grew to like Madeira wine so much that it was used to toast the signing of the Declaration of Independence in 1776. The lucrative

Catherine of Braganza (above) and sightseeing by hammock (left)

trade also helped establish some of the island's oldest merchant families, such as the Blandys and the Leacocks, who are still very much in business today.

Foreign tourists have also had a major impact on the island, whether coming for the good of their health, or escaping from the cold northern European winter, or stopping *en route* to India, the Far East, South Africa or

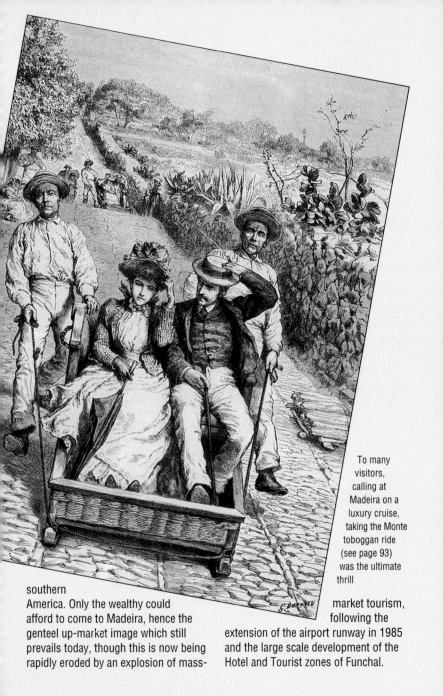

To many visitors, calling at Madeira on a luxury cruise, taking the Monte toboggan ride (see page 93) was the ultimate thrill

southern America. Only the wealthy could afford to come to Madeira, hence the genteel up-market image which still prevails today, though this is now being rapidly eroded by an explosion of mass-market tourism, following the extension of the airport runway in 1985 and the large scale development of the Hotel and Tourist zones of Funchal.

THE ENGLISH CHURCH AND BRITISH CEMETERY

Madeira's English church is a circular domed building in neo-classical style which opened in 1822. The architect was Madeira's British Consul, Henry Veitch, who had to work within the constraints of Catholic Portuguese law. This reluctantly allowed the Protestant community on Madeira to build a place of worship, so long as it did not look like a church. The galleried interior is light and airy, lit by fan-shaped windows around the base of the dome, and brightened by fine flower arrangements. Surrounding the church is a well-tended garden containing a bust of Philippa of Lancaster, daughter of John of Gaunt and mother of Prince Henry the Navigator, whose marriage to King João I of Portugal in 1387 established the long-standing Portuguese–British alliance. Attached to the nearby chaplaincy is a library of some 2,500 volumes in English, which is open to visitors.

The British Cemetery is a short walk away, a beautiful and poignant spot full of flowers, lizards, birds and butterflies. Opened in 1887, it contains moving memorials to Protestants of all nations, not just the British. Many record the short lives of hopeful visitors who came to Madeira in search of relief from consumptive diseases but did not long survive. You can also read memorials to several of the German, Polish, Danish and American physicians who came here to treat them.

The English Church, Rua do Quebra Costas 18. Open: dawn until dusk. Services: see pages 185–6.
The British Cemetery, Rua da Carreira 235. Open: daylight hours (ring the bell at the gate for entry).

IBTAM HANDICRAFTS INSTITUTE

Crafts are such an important part of the Madeiran economy that this institute was set up to provide training and monitor standards. It is principally concerned with the arts of embroidery, tapestry and wickerwork and a small museum on the first floor of the institute's headquarters building displays some very fine examples of all three. Climbing the stairs to the museum you will be greeted by a massive tapestry, *The Allegory of Madeira*, designed by Gino Ramoli and made between 1958 and 1961. The tapestry, depicting a typically flower-filled Madeiran landscape, contains a total of 7 million stitches, the work of 14 girls. The museum itself consists of cases full of embroidered tablecloths, bedspreads and diaphanous nightgowns all of which will appeal to the connoisseur of fine needlework. Also on display are some interesting examples of island costume, including colourful hand-embroidered waistcoats, blouses and scarves, and a small exhibition showing how embroidery designs are transferred, using inked rollers, to the fabric before the embroiderers begin their work.
Rua do Visconde de Anadia 44. Open: Monday to Friday, 9am–12.30pm and 2pm–5.30pm. Admission free.

IGREJA DO COLÉGIO

The baroque façade of this collegiate church dominates Funchal's main square, though it is not the most attractive on Madeira, and the gesticulating Jesuit saints filling the niches look in danger of toppling over in their frenzy of religious ecstasy. The interior is more likeable with its geometric *azulejos* tiles, and its altar surrounds carved in gilded wood and

Colourful contrasts: the façade of the Jesuit church fronting Funchal's main square

plaster, featuring fat pink cherubs climbing through a tangle of vineleaves. The decoration mostly dates from the period 1641 to 1660 though the church itself was founded in 1574, soon after the Jesuits were granted permission to establish a college, or seminary, on Madeira. After the Jesuits were expelled from Portugal in 1759, the college was turned into a military barracks but more recently it has been designated part of Madeira's embryonic university.

Praça do Município. Open: daily, 5pm–6pm and for services.

EMBROIDERY

The art of embroidery was introduced to Madeira by Elizabeth Phelps, daughter of a British wine shipper, during the 1850s, a time of particular calamity on Madeira: cholera struck the island in 1852, carrying off 7,000 victims, and disease devastated the vine crops later in the same year. The resulting poverty so distressed Miss Phelps that she established her embroidery business as a means of supplementing the islanders' meagre incomes. The samples Miss Phelps took to London were warmly received and by 1862 there were 1,000 women employed in the business. Today that number has grown to 20,000, but it remains a cottage-based industry. Whole families, including men and boys, are involved, and the embroiderers love to tell the cautionary tale of a husband and wife team who together worked a huge tablecloth, starting at opposite ends. Only when the work was well advanced did they discover that the husband was sewing one face of the cloth, his wife the other. You can understand how easily this might happen if you visit one of the island's several embroidery 'factories' where the designs are pricked out on to the linen before it is sent to outworkers and where, once the embroiderers have finished their work, the cloth is finished, washed, ironed and then given the special IBTAM seal. This metal tag, found on all genuine Madeiran embroidery, is a guarantee of authenticity granted by the island's handicrafts institute (see page 36). It also guarantees a high price, since Madeiran embroidery is far from cheap, but you will understand why once you have seen the quality of the work and the beauty of the intricate floral designs.

Thousands of hours of meticulous work go into the design, production and finishing of Madeiran embroidery

Jardim Botânico

*T*he whole of Madeira is one vast botanical garden where plants grow in extraordinary profusion, thanks to the combination of fertile volcanic soils, sunshine, regular rainfall and high humidity. If you are interested in plants, the Botanical Garden is the place to come to learn more about the island's exotic flora. Even if you are not a plant buff, you will enjoy the magnificent setting and the views.

Natural History Museum

The Botanical Garden first opened to the public in 1960. Before that it had been a private estate appropriately called the Quinta do Bom Successo (Good Fortune Estate) belonging to the Reid family, founders of Reid's Hotel (see page 172).

The Reids' former residence now houses a Natural History Museum located just inside the entrance gates. This contains cases full of fossils, fish,

insects and stuffed birds – all of which look rather dusty with age and far from lifelike. There are, however, one or two more impressive exhibits, such as the massive piece of fossilised tree heather (*Erica scoparia*) which would have grown to an even greater girth had its life not been ended by volcanic eruptions 10 million years ago.

The Garden

Immediately around the museum is an area devoted to orchids (in flower from

All done with colourful foliage

November to March). Another area is planted with species indigenous to Madeira – plants which are not found anywhere else in the world in the wild. Some of these have, of course, been disseminated by botanists and horticulturalists to other parts of the world since their original discovery, including the *Geranium maderense* (Madeiran cranesbill) with its handsome ferny foliage and masses of magenta flowers. Paths radiate from the museum to various points of the garden. If you want to explore the site systematically, climb to the top of the garden first, to the so-called Lovers' Grotto and viewpoint. Once this *miradouro* overlooked a deep green ravine; it still does, but the foreground is now filled with the sight of the island's new expressway under construction. When the elevated section, on massive concrete stilts, is finally completed the gardens are less likely to be the tranquil refuge from city life that they are today.

From this high point, a series of terraces descends down the hillside to an open-air café, set amid carp-filled ponds and rampant stands of papyrus grass. The lower terraces are more regimented than the woodland areas higher up – indeed, one area is devoted to commercial plants grown for the cut-flower trade and as seasonal bedding.

The bedding plants are planted in geometric patterns designed to show off their foliage colours, ranging from sulphur yellow to grey and deep purple; one block even spells out *Benvindo* (welcome) in beetroot red. After this the sparse simplicity of the cactus and succulent beds comes as something of a relief to the eye. If you are lucky, some of these splendid and massive plants will be in flower, the exotic colours of the

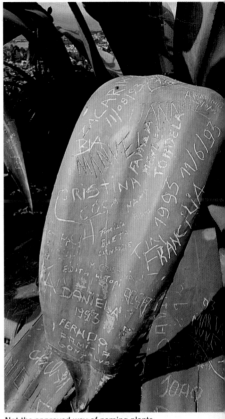
Not the approved way of naming plants

blossoms contrasting with the sculptural simplicity of the trunk and branches. Even if there are no blossoms, the dense and intricate cobwebs threaded between the prickly leaves provide the oportunity for close study of the island's spider population.

Caminho do Meio (on the outskirts of Funchal). Open: gardens daily, 9am–6pm; museum daily, 9am–12.30pm and 1.30–5.30pm. Admission charge. Bus 30 from Funchal or taxi.

The African Tulip Tree, or Flame of the Forest, blooms in the Jardim dos Loiros

JARDIM DOS LOIROS

While exploring the Jardim Botânico (page 40) you will hear a constant chorus of hoots, whoops and screeches emanating from the adjacent property. If your curiosity is aroused you can discover the source of all this noise by taking a short downhill walk from the entrance to the Botanical Garden to the Jardim dos Loiros (Tropical Bird Garden). Here, amid well-tended gardens, some of the birds roam free but most are displayed in aviaries dotted around the grounds. The various cockatoos, parrots and parakeets are as gaudily coloured as the flowers and some reveal even more striking colours when they open their wings to fly. You will enjoy the sight of these colourful birds so long as your conscience is not troubled by the knowledge that they are kept in such an unstimulating environment. A bare concrete cage is a long way from the treetops of the South American jungle.

Caminho do Meio. Open: daily, 9am–6pm. Admission charge. Bus 30 or taxi from Funchal.

JARDIM ORQUÍDEA

This tiny garden, located some 200m from the Jardim Botânico (page 40) allows you to view the different processes involved in commercial orchid production. During the orchid flowering season (from the end of November to early April) the shade houses and polythene tunnels are full of exotic blooms – some spidery, some fat and waxy, spotted or plain and in every colour from brown, black and purple to electric blue, yellow and green. For the rest of the year, the garden is not one of Madeira's most compelling attractions unless you are an orchid fanatic because there is little to see except for displays covering the propagation and development of orchid seeds.

Rua Pita da Silva, 37. Open: daily, 8am–6pm. Admission charge. Bus 30 or taxi from Funchal.

JARDIM DE SANTA CATARINA

If you walk to central Funchal from the Hotel Zone on a regular basis you will soon get to know this public park on the hillside overlooking the harbour. A mini botanical garden, it contains a number of fine specimen trees planted in the late 1940s when the garden was converted from a disused cemetery. Fountains and aviaries dot the park as well as some industrial relics – a steamroller and a sugar-cane mill, for example.

There is also an open-air café and a children's adventure playground. A bronze sculpture of a sower, the work of Francisco Franco (page 50), stands on the main lawn of the park, whilst lower down, near the Capela de Santa Catarina, is a statue of Christopher Columbus and a modernistic fountain featuring a prone female torso. The chapel itself dates from 1425, built on the orders of Zarco's wife, Constança Rodriguez, and is the oldest place of worship on Madeira. The body of the little chapel has been rebuilt several times, most recently in the 17th century, but the porch shelters the original holy water stoup, carved with the wheel of St Catherine.

Avenida do Infante. Open 24 hours.

JARDIM DE SÃO FRANCISCO

This most central of Funchal's public gardens offers a shady retreat close to the Tourist Information Centre and is a popular place where Madeirans, young and old, meet to gossip and pass the time of day. It also contains some magnificent trees (most of which are labelled) planted in the 19th century, when Franciscan monks, along with all religious orders, were expelled from Portugal. This garden was created for public use on the site of their ruined convent, and amid the lush foliage you can still see the stone-carved coat of arms which once decorated the convent gateway.

Avenida Arriaga. Open: 24 hours.

Symbol of Madeira's fertility, Franco's statue of the *Semeador*, the Sower

MERCADO DOS LAVRADORES

The Workers' Market is one of the most compelling and colourful sights on Madeira, a bustling place which touches on all aspects of island life, not just food. Friday is the best day to go because peasant farmers from all over the island come to the market on that day, bringing their produce for sale. Makeshift stalls are set up in the streets and in the car park to the south of Rua de Carlos I. Even if you do not want to shop, the market is worth visiting for the magnificent displays, especially those of

the costumed flowersellers at the entrance to the covered market, and those of the fruit and vegetable vendors on the ground floor. Those who are squeamish about the sight of fish being gutted and filleted should, perhaps, give the basement fish market a miss. The prices, both for fruit and for fish, are extraordinarily low, and you will soon realise why most of the island's farmers have to survive on a very meagre income. Even so, most market traders usually find a few *escudos* to spare when the lottery ticket sellers do their rounds of the market, offering the chance to win that dream ticket to end all financial worries.

Produce to tempt all the senses, on sale in the bustling Workers' Market

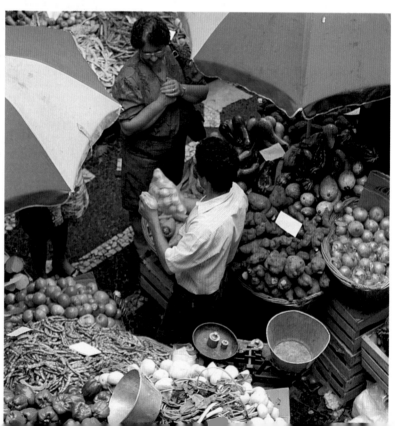

MUSEU DE ARTE SACRA

The pride of Madeira's Museum of Religious Art is a small collection of top quality Flemish paintings good enough to grace even the world's leading art museums. The paintings were commissioned in the 15th and 16th centuries by patrons who amassed extraordinary wealth in Madeira's highly profitable sugar trade. Little is known about the painters who created these works: cities such as Antwerp, where the pictures were probably painted, had a large number of professional artists who worked to order. Originally these paintings were placed above the main altar in churches all over the island but they have now been gathered into this museum for safety. The museum is housed in the former bishop's palace, built in 1600 and remodelled between 1748 and 1757.

The one-way route round the museum ensures that the best is kept until last. First you are directed to the upper rooms full of embroidered vestments, illuminated hymn books in tooled leather bindings and carved reliefs in painted and gilded wood. Some of the religious statues are sickly sweet but two exhibits stand out: the 16th-century Virgin and Child in Room 2 and the intricately decorated processional cross in Room 6–7. Both of these were given to the island by the Portuguese king, Manuel I, who reigned from 1490 to 1520.

Downstairs, splendidly exhibited, are the 19 paintings that form the highlights of the museum, skilfully restored to bring out the full impact of their rich colours.

Flemish art, paid for by sugar wealth, in the Museum of Sacred Art

Several take the form of a triptych – three-part pictures showing a religious subject in the central panel and portraits of the kneeling donors, with their patron saints, on the two side panels. Perhaps the best example is the *Deposition* (or Descent from the Cross) flanked by fine portraits of Simon Acciaiuoli, an Italian merchant, and his wife. Another shows Saints James and Philip flanked by members of the family of Simon Gonçalves da Câmara, the grandson of Zarco, Madeira's discoverer.

Rua do Bispo 21. Open: Tuesday to Saturday, 10am–12.30pm and 2.30pm–5.20pm; Sunday 10am–1pm (but parts of the museum may be closed for renovation in the near future). Admission charge.

ISLAND COSTUME

The flowersellers of Funchal's Mercado dos Lavradores (see page 44) all wear the distinctive costume of the island. For women this means a striped woollen skirt worn with a red embroidered waistcoat, beautiful pleated blouse and a shoulder scarf. Red is the dominant colour, but the scarlet stripes of the skirt alternate with yellow, black, green, blue or white stripes – the precise colour combinations differ from one village to another, as do the embroidery patterns on the scarf and waistcoat. Similarly the colours in the waist sash worn by the men provide a clue to their home village. The sash is worn with a white linen shirt and baggy knee-length trousers. You will often see men wearing bobble hats as

Madeiran costume is as bright as the island's flowers

you tour the island, knitted with ear-flaps as a precaution against the cold winds that can blow above 800m. For special occasions both men and women wear the *carapuça*, a small black or blue

Soft, supple boots enable Madeirans to walk long distances

skull cap with a long tassel. Both sexes also wear boots called *botacha*. These are made of naturally tanned cowhide and goatskin with the upper part turned down to the ankles and trimmed with a red band. Madeiran song and folk dance groups, who regularly perform in Funchal's hotels and restaurants, take their art very seriously and aim to keep island customs alive – they will show you and explain different parts of their costume and there is a small display of authentic historical costume, showing regional variations, in the IBTAM museum (see page 36).

(see page 36)

Wind protection (left) and toboggan guide's boater (right)

MUSEU DE CIDADE

The City Museum tracing the history of Funchal from the city's foundations to the present day, is housed on the upper floor of the Câmara Municipal, or Town Hall. This is one of the island's most handsome buildings, originally built towards the end of the 18th century as a private mansion by one of Madeira's wealthiest residents, the second Conde (Count) de Carvalhal. The city's old town hall was demolished in 1913 amid popular rejoicing – it had come to symbolise the absolutist and backward-looking rule of the Portuguese monarchy which was finally overthrown by the Republican Revolution of 1910. Despite the conversion of this building to administrative purposes, it retains the atmosphere of a private family house.

The courtyard, or patio, is especially delightful with its cobbled paving, palm trees and *azulejos* tiles, not to mention the merrily splashing fountain surmounted by an intimate sculpture of *Leda and the Swan* (1880). There is also a lovely view looking back towards the Praça do Município, taking in the intersecting arches of the external staircase linking the three floors of the building.

The City Museum's Leda fountain

The museum is located on the first floor and you are guided by a timeline running round the walls, recording key dates in Funchal's history, beginning with the discovery of Madeira in 1420 and the peopling of the city from 1425 (the first children born on the island were twins who were baptised, appropriately enough, Adam and Eve).

Exhibits hung on the walls above the timeline or displayed in nearby cabinets include early sugar moulds (which also feature on the city's coat of arms), weights and measures, model ships and photographs of the city's earliest surviving buildings. Machico (see page 88) was originally designated as the island's capital, but Funchal developed more rapidly because of its deep natural harbour. During the reign of King Manuel I (1490–1520), Funchal began to take on its capital city status, with the building of the Customs House, now the island's parliament building (see page 32) and the cathedral (page 56–7). The subsequent growth of the city is recorded in paintings (including a superb panoramic view painted in 1777) and hand-engraved maps. More recent history is recorded in photographs: some of them show the damage caused by a German

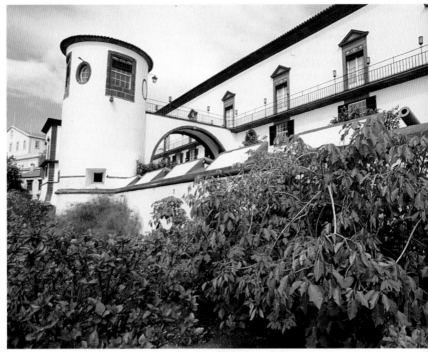

Cannons poke out over the poinsettia-clad walks of the São Lourenço fortress

submarine which bombarded Funchal in World War I in an unsuccessful attempt to prevent the island being used as a support base for Atlantic shipping; others commemorate famous visitors to the island, from King Charles of Portugal (1901) to Pope John Paul II (1991). *Praça do Município. Open: Monday to Friday, 9am–12.30pm and 2pm–5pm. Admission free.*

MUSEU FORTALEZA

The Fortress Museum is located within the bastions of the Palácio de São Lourenço entered through a splendid 16th-century carved stone portal. The museum traces the history of the fortress from its construction in the 1520s to its later conversion into the official residence of the island's two governors – one military, one civilian. On display are historic guns, cannon, armour and photographs of the palace as it is today, complete with titillating 19th-century ceiling frescos of Neptune and a retinue of blowzy mermaids. Photographs are as close as you can get to the main building which is still the residence of Madeira's armed forces' Commander-in-Chief and guarded by goose-stepping, sword-carrying soldiers. *Avenida Arriaga (opposite the tourist information office). Open: officially daily, 10am–noon and 2pm–6pm, but in reality whenever the army chooses. Admission free.*

MUSEU FRANCO

Art lovers should make the effort to see
this excellent but quiet museum
displaying the work of the two Franco de
Sousa brothers. Henrique (1883–1961)
was a painter and Francisco
(1855–1955) was a sculptor. Though
born on Madeira, both spent much of
their lives working in Lisbon and in
Paris, where they were much influenced
by the artistic milieu of Picasso, Degas
and Modigliani. Henrique experimented
with various styles, so there are canvases

Gauguinesque portraits by Henrique Franco de
Sousa celebrating the tropical richness of
Madeira

here that will remind you of Van Gogh,
Gauguin and Cézanne, but he eventually
found his forte as a portrait painter; his
pictures are fresh, colourful and airy and
he endows all his sitters with character
and nobility, be they peasants with
weatherworn faces or pampered
aristocrats seated in their gardens.
Francisco is the better known simply
because his statues, such as the Zarco
monument marking the centre of
Funchal, and the *Semeador* (Sower) in
the Jardim de Santa Catarina, are
familiar city landmarks. The displays
covering his work include
commemorative statues, working
drawings, lithographs and designs for
medals, coins and postage stamps.
*Rua do João de Deus 13. Open: daily,
9am–12.30pm and 2pm–5.30pm.
Admission free.*

MUSEU FREDERICO DE FREITAS

This absorbing museum is in two parts but is still in the process of arrangement, so details may change. The first part consists of hundreds of cartoons, engravings and paintings of Madeira, most of them dating from the 19th century, hung round the walls of a two-storey gallery. The eyes glaze over after a while faced with such a mass of material, much of which derives from the hand of amateur artists. Even so, it is interesting to see how these artists have responded to the island's dramatic landscapes, which are so different in their elemental force from the gutter pastoral scenes that there artists were trained to draw. There is also an amusing sequence of pictures by Isabella de França from the journal she kept on her visit to Portugal and Madeira in 1853–4. Isabella herself was honest enough to admit that her paintings were somewhat crude, but they do record what she experienced with frankness and humour.

All these pictures were bequeathed to Madeira in 1978 by the lawyer Dr Frederico de Freitas, along with his house, which forms the second part of the museum. This charming old residence was built in the late 17th century by the Counts of Calçada, but with splendid art nouveau additions, including the little *salon vitré* (conservatory) in the garden designed for sitting in and admiring the views, and the intimate Winter Garden, with its cane furniture, doors and hanging lamp all in the art nouveau style.

The stately rooms are crammed with objects collected by Dr de Freitas, from fine furniture, carpets and religious paintings to an extraordinary collection of some 2,000 jugs. There is also an important collection of handpainted *azulejos* tiles but the most endearing items are the crib figures and Madonnas carved in wood in the 17th and 18th centuries, some from the distant outposts of the Portuguese empire, such as Goa and Macao.

Calçada Santa Clara. Open: Tuesday to Sunday, 10am–12.30pm and 2pm–6pm. Admission free.

The inviting art nouveau interior of the Freitas Winter Garden

MUSEU MUNICIPAL

The Municipal Museum is much more fun than the rather bureaucratic name suggests, consisting of an aquarium downstairs and displays of stuffed sharks, as well as birds, mammals and other forms of Madeiran wildlife upstairs. Younger children will enjoy staring into the gaping jaws of the sharks and imagining what it might be like to be munched by those perfectly vicious razor-sharp teeth. There are plenty more ugly-looking specimens to feed you nightmares, including bloated prickly porcupine fish and a giant crab with claws almost a metre long. Some of the displays are very realistic; some of the island's birds are shown as if feeding their young in the nest surrounded by all the debris and droppings you would expect. The aquarium below is pitch dark except for the large tanks containing typical Madeiran fish and marine vegetation. Try spotting the flounders, masters of camouflage, wonder at the beauty of the sea anemones and see how crabs walk under water – balletically on the tips of their claws watched by brooding surly lobsters and weird beasts such as the scorpion fish. Altogether this museum is a good introduction to the island's wildlife as well as being a good distraction for passing a rainy hour or so. *Rua da Mouraria 31. Open: Tuesday to Friday, 10am–6pm; Saturday and Sunday, noon–6pm. Admission free.*

MUSEU PHOTOGRAPHIA VICENTES

This tiny museum is set within the cramped photographic studio of Vicente Gomes da Silva, set up in 1856 as the first commercial photographic business not just in Madeira, but in all Portugal. The studio survives intact, complete with its heavy 19th-century furnishings, its early plate cameras of mahogany and

Submarine encounters at the Municipal Museum: groper fish meets Moray eels

Tea in the patio: the gracious courtyard of the Vicentes Photographic Museum

brass and its miniature stage – this theatrical device, with its sliding scenery and props, allowed clients to choose their own background, so that they could be photographed either in the streets of Funchal, or amid mountain ravines, or seated in a grandly decorated salon, all by simply moving a piece of realistically painted canvas.

Having taken all this in – and it doesn't take long, unless you have an absorbing interest in old cameras – the museum custodians will then suggest that you take a seat and thumb through the photographic albums. These contain a selection of pictures taken by Gomes da Silva, by his son and by two of his grandchildren who inherited the business, and they provide an absorbing account of life on Madeira spanning the period from 1856 until the business closed in 1973. The more familiar you already are with Madeira, the more

absorbing you will find these pictures, because you will be able to compare the scene then with your knowledge of what it looks like now. The portraits range from royal visitors and society beauties to children and dogs; there are 1920s views of plump matrons being carried in hammocks by handsome moustachioed porters in straw hats, of bullock carts and toboggans. There are also pictures of tall-masted sailing ships crowding Funchal harbour, of barrels of Madeira being loaded into the holds and of hardworking porters carrying great loads using wooden yokes. As a documentary history of the island, the museum is a rich treasure house, and in years to come the government intends to exhibit many more of the 380,000 or so photographs in the collection (most until now unseen by the public).

Rua da Carreira 43. Open: Monday to Friday, 2pm–6pm. Admission charge.

Museu Quinta das Cruzes

*T*he Quinta das Cruzes (literally 'The Mansion of the Crosses') is an elegant and airy house which gives a taste of the lifestyle once enjoyed by Madeira's most wealthy inhabitants. It is said that Grande Capitaõ Zarco, Madeira's discoverer and Funchal's first ruler, had his house on this site, splendidly situated high on a hill above the city.

Now the house is surrounded by suburbs, though the world is kept at bay by the high garden wall and the extensive gardens which have been designated as an 'archaeological park'. This means that 15th- and 16th-century tombstones, coats of arms, architectural mouldings and inscriptions have been placed around the garden where rampant vegetation obscures much of their detail but adds to their romantic charm.

The two most striking exhibits are the

Man-eating beasts and their prey: detail from a Manueline window frame

huge stone window frames set on the lawn to the left of the museum entrance, carved with little man-eating lions, dancing figures and rope motifs. Some would have you believe that these come from the house in which Christopher Columbus lived on Madeira (see page 13); in fact they date from 1517 and are a fine example of the ornate Manueline style which flourished under the reign of Manuel I of Portugal (1490–1520). In the rest of the garden you will find frog-filled ponds, dragon trees (*Dracaena draco*) with claw-like aerial roots and bark like the skin of a reptile, and a big display of pot-grown orchids (in flower from late November to early April).

The present house largely dates from the early 19th century when the original 17th-century structure was rebuilt by the Lomelino family, wealthy Genoese wine shippers, who furnished it in the typical style of the period. There are many delicate pieces of furniture in the Regency Trafalgar style, made from the local *vinhático* wood (*Persea indica*), similar in colour to mahogany, as well as pieces by Chippendale and Hepplewhite which the owners of the mansion may have purchased from visiting tourists; it was the practice, in the 19th century, for visitors overwintering on the island to bring their own furniture and then sell it off at the end of their stay to pay the rent, as well as the servants' wages and the grocer's bills.

Each room of the mansion has a different theme, which you will discover as you explore. **Room 4** contains art from India and China, imported by the Portuguese East India Company, notably a watery blue silk wall-hanging embroidered with butterflies from northern India and a rare Cizhou-ware vase, made in China in the 13th century. European art features in **Room 5**, including a Flemish painting by Jean de Mabuse of the *Three Magi* (1470). A huge 18th-century Aubusson carpet and a tapestry of similar date, featuring dancing peasants, sets the theme for the French style of **Room 6**. In **Room 9** do not miss the big oil painting of Funchal, one of several topographical views set about the house. **Room 10** contains 19th-century costumes and jewellery – everything from full dress uniforms to lace and linen nightclothes – and in **Room 11** there are some tender crib figures of painted clay, made in the 18th

Embroidered silk from India

and 19th centuries. **Downstairs**, in the former kitchens and basements, is a miscellaneous collection including a series of satirical lithographs poking fun at Madeiran dress and manners – especially those of the clergy, who are portrayed as fat and self-indulgent. Here, too, are finds from the Dutch East India ship, the *Slot ter Hooge*, wrecked off Porto Santo in 1724 and excavated in 1974. Finally there are some fine examples of cupboards made out of recycled packing cases – not today's flimsy affairs, but 17th-century packing cases made of stout hardwoods which, once Madeira's sugar trade died, were taken apart and made into furniture.

Calçada do Pico 1. Open: garden, Tuesday to Sunday, 10am–6pm (admission free); house, Tuesday to Sunday, 10am–12.30pm and 2pm–6pm (admission charge Tuesday to Saturday; free on Sunday).

QUINTA DA BOA VISTA

The Quinta da Boa Vista, sometimes referred to by its old name, the Garton Greenhouses, is well worth visiting if you are interested in plants and gardens. The Quinta specialises in growing orchids for the cut-flower market, propagating the microscopic seeds (each seed head can produce 5 million seeds) and nurturing them through the critical first four years of their life until the tiny plants are ready to be taken out of their test tubes and exposed to the open air. Extraordinarily delicate in the early years, they then become unbelievably tough – surviving, seemingly, in dust-dry soil with no visible means of nutrition. Being epiphytes, they derive their nourishment from moisture in the air, and Madeira's humid climate provides ideal living conditions. Though most orchids only flower in winter (the first blooms appear in late November

Exotics of the plant world: a carefully nurtured Quinta da Boa Vista orchid

and the flowering period continues until early April), the lovingly tended gardens around the Quinta da Boa Vista make a visit worthwhile at any time of year. You can also buy orchids and flowers to take home (see Shopping, page 146).
Rua Luis Figueiroa Albuquerque. Open: Monday to Saturday, 9am–5.30pm.

SÉ (Cathedral)

Funchal's cathedral was begun in 1485 and completed in 1514. Its construction marked a major stage in Funchal's development. Previously it had been a small frontier town at the edge of the known world, a place full of adventurers, slaves and refugees, beyond the reach of law and religion. Now it was thought worthy of a cathedral and the king of Portugal himself, Manuel I, sent two master-builders to supervise the work, along with the gift of a fine processional cross (now in the Museu de Arte Sacra – see page 45).

Naturally enough the cathedral was built in the Manueline style, named after the king, a late Gothic development noted for inventive decorations – these reflected nautical themes (anchors, ropes, fish) and the kind of strange birds, animals and flowers that Portuguese explorers were beginning to see in newly discovered areas of the world. The playful Manueline details of Funchal's cathedral are best seen from the streets to the south of the church, looking up to the barley-sugar pinnacles rising from the roof near the tower. Equally exotic are the designs on the nave ceiling, though these are difficult to see in the very dark interior: they are picked out in white ivory against a background of carved wood from the native Madeiran tree, variously known as juniper or prickly cedar (*Juniperus cedrus*). If the cathedral

A typical Madeiran carved and gilded altar frame in Funchal cathedral

doors are open they may emit just enough light to let you view the choir stalls, carved out of the same wood and painted blue and gold. The stalls depict saints, apostles and evangelists but in the clothing of the 17th century, when they were carved, and so providing an insight into contemporary (male) fashion. Sadly, even with the doors open you will have to take it on trust that the altar is surrounded by 16th-century Flemish and Portuguese paintings – it really is too dark to see, though you can get an idea of the rich splendour if you come here when the chancel is lit up for a service, or for the occasional classical concerts which take advantage of the cathedral's fine acoustics.

Rua do Aljube. Open: daily during daylight hours. Admission free.

EXPLORING CHURCHES

Madeira is still a very religious island, and large sums of money are spent on maintaining and restoring parish churches. Sadly, for the architectural historian, this means that most have been rebuilt several times since their original foundation and the present structures seem to be of no great age, with their bland neo-baroque façades and interiors. If you dig around, however, you may find a few features that are older and more interesting. Here are some pointers and clues as to where to look.

First seek out the font at the back of the church – usually housed in a small room, or baptistry, to the north (left as you enter the church). The font is likely to be the oldest surviving feature, because churches have often been rebuilt but the parish will retain the original 15th-century font as a link with the original community. Some are plain hollowed-out boulders, while others (such as the one in Ribeira Brava: see page 106) are more ornately carved. The main altar is likely to be the next oldest feature, and although the statuary may

Modern mass-produced statuary and *azulejos* tiles are typical of many Madeiran churches

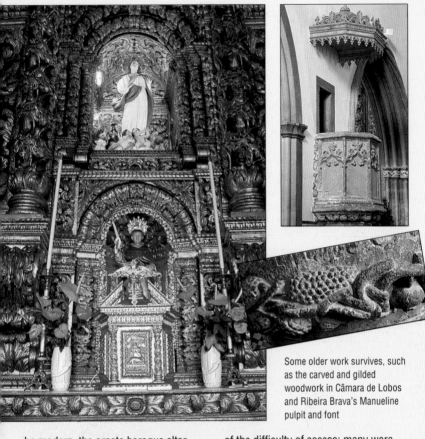

Some older work survives, such as the carved and gilded woodwork in Câmara de Lobos and Ribeira Brava's Manueline pulpit and font

be modern, the ornate baroque altar surround, often of carved and gilded wood, usually dates to the 17th or 18th century and is full of fascinating little details, such as cherubs and butterflies hidden amid a mass of vine leaves and foliage. The walls of the church may be covered in *azulejos* tiles of similar date – usually handpainted in soft blues and yellows in complex geometric patterns. Pictorial tiles showing scenes from the life of Christ are likely to be more modern and mass produced. Ceilings do not get repainted very often because of the difficulty of access; many were last painted in the early part of this century, if not earlier, and floral patterns are common, usually incorporating examples of Madeira's abundant wild flora. Every church on Madeira has something of interest if you look hard enough, even if it is not of great age. A favourite with many visitors is the fishermen's chapel in Câmara de Lobos (see page 80) whose walls are painted with charmingly naïve pictures of the miracles of St Nicholas, patron saint of seafarers.

To the Waterfront

If you have just arrived in Madeira, this walk is for you. It is designed to give you a route from the Hotel Zone to central Funchal. *At a leisurely pace it will take you between 30 minutes and an hour.*

Estrada Monumental, the main road through the Hotel Zone, is very busy because it takes all the traffic leaving Funchal for the west of the island. A new expressway, linking Funchal to Ribeira Brava, is under construction and will eventually take most of the traffic away – for now, put up with the noise and try and enjoy the views towards Funchal, which are especially good around Reid's Hotel (see page 172). From here descend Avenida do Infante.

1 AVENIDA DO INFANTE

You will pass some fine art deco villas on the left-hand side while on the right is the Savoy Hotel and then the modern Casino Park Hotel. The circular casino in the grounds is shaped like a crown and was designed in the 1970s by Oscar Niemeyer, best known for his work in the Brazilian capital, Brasília.

Next on the right comes a mansion painted bougainvillea pink and protected by an armed guard – this is the Quinta Vigia, the official residence of Madeira's president.

Cross to the opposite side of the road and look for the entrance to the Hospício da Princesa.

2 HOSPÍCIO DA PRINCESA

Very few visitors ever find their way into the well-tended gardens of this hospital, though they are open to the public. The hospital itself dates from 1859 when it was founded as a sanatorium for tuberculosis sufferers by Doña Amelia, wife of Emperor Pedro I of Brazil, as a memorial to their daughter who died from the disease.

Cross the road again to enter the Jardim de Santa Catarina.

3 JARDIM DE SANTA CATARINA

This small park will provide you with a good introduction to the botanical richness of Madeira, for it is planted with a good variety of flowering trees and shrubs, some of them labelled. At the centre of the park is the 1919 bronze statue of the *Semeador*, the Sower, scattering seed across the lawns.

To the right of the park there are good views down over the harbour and central Funchal. Paths lead down to the Capela de Santa Catarina, said to have been built in 1425 by Constança Rodriguez, wife of Zarco, the island's discoverer. It is thus Madeira's oldest church, but the venerable building is always locked and wears an air of neglect. Looking down from the terrace where the chapel sits, you can see the traffic roundabout known as the Rotunda do Infante. Here is a statue of Henry the Navigator seated beneath a rather ugly

stone arch and looking across to a fountain of seahorses supporting a globe (the Central Funchal walk, see page 62, begins here).

Keep over to the right-hand side of the park and a flight of steps will take you down to Avenida do Mar.

4 AVENIDA DO MAR

Those who like boats and marine life will enjoy watching the waterside activities in Funchal's harbour – with luck a huge ocean-going cruise liner will be in port or a tall-masted sailing ship. You will also see cargo being unloaded from container ships and boats being repaired. Further along Avenida do Mar is the yacht marina, lined by good seafood restaurants on the landward side. Just before you reach the floating restaurant, turn right and walk out along the sea wall surrounding the marina. This is well worth doing for the views back to the island, and for the colourful graffiti painted on the walls by the many people who have sailed to Madeira in the yachts from America or other parts of Europe.

From here you can join The Old Town walk (see page 64), simply by continuing along the waterfront to the Praça da Autonomia.

Sailors' graffiti in the yachting marina

São
Vicente
• Rabaçal   *Pico do*   Ponta de São
             Arieiro   Lourenço
                 Quinta do
Ribeira •   ▲ Palheiro
Brava   Funchal

Central Funchal

Funchal's main avenue, Avenida Arriaga, was laid out at the turn of the century with a wide central carriageway, shaded by trees and equipped with benches, where Madeirans come to stroll and gossip, especially in the evenings. The avenue is lined with noble buildings, shops and art galleries. *Allow 2 hours.*

Start at the Rotunda do Infante, at the western end of Avenida Arriaga.

1 ROTUNDA DO INFANTE

The roundabout is named after the Infante, or Prince, Henry the Navigator who never visited Madeira but sent Zarco to claim the island for Portugal in 1420. The newly opened Marina Shopping Centre on the right is full of up-market shops and is popular with cruise passengers.

Take the next turning right, Rua do Conselheiro José Silvestre

Ribeiro, to the Casa do Turista at the bottom on the left.

2 CASA DO TURISTA

The Casa do Turista, or, as it styles itself, 'The Famous Shop', is more like a museum than a shop, an elegantly furnished town house where all sorts of tempting displays of embroidery and tableware are laid out beneath ornately plastered ceilings. The shop stocks top-quality crafts not just from Madeira but also from mainland Portugal.

Return up Rua do Conselheiro and turn right to the Teatro Municipal.

3 TEATRO MUNICIPAL

The Municipal Theatre was built in 1888 and has boxes rising vertically in tiers, modelled on the Little Theatre at Versailles. Often there is an art exhibition in the foyer which enables you to go in and look around. The theatre bar, open to the street with its tree-shaded garden area, is a popular meeting place among Bohemian Madeirans.

Next to the theatre is an even more ornate building, now a Toyota showroom, decorated with _azulejos_ tiles showing visitors to the island in the 1920s being carried in a hammock and riding a toboggan from Monte. Opposite is the colourful Jardim de São Francisco (see page 42), a garden full of tropical trees and shrubs built on the site of the former Franciscan friary, closed in 1834.

4 PALÁCIO DE SÃO LOURENÇO

The next building on the right, with bulky cream-coloured walls, is the St Lawrence Palace, built in the 16th century to defend Funchal from pirate attacks and still the headquarters of Madeira's military command. Sword-bearing soldiers guard the main entrance

but there is a small museum open to the public (see page 49). Opposite is the Tourist Information Centre and the Adegas (Wine Lodge) de São Francisco, well worth visiting (see page 28).

5 MONUMENTO A JOÃO GONÇALVES ZARCO

Just beyond the palace, the Zarco monument marks the heart of Funchal. The statue of the island's discoverer was carved by the Madeiran sculptor, Francisco Franco (see page 50) and unveiled in 1934. On the northwestern corner of the square is the splendid Banco de Portugal building, one of the best in the city with the decorative details of swags, baskets of fruit and human figures carved in marble and grey basalt contrasting with the gleaming white walls.

Across Avenida Zarco is the regional government building with its huge tiled entrance hall and courtyard fountain, while the next building along, the Banco Nacional Ultramarino, has a pretty art deco lamp on its entrance stair consisting of a bronze maiden symbolising commerce.

6 SÉ (CATHEDRAL)

Avenida Arriaga ends at the cathedral (see page 56) on whose north side flowersellers dressed in scarlet embroidered costumes have their stalls (from here you can join the Between the Rivers walk, page 66). To the south and east lie a warren of little alleys, whose shops are gradually being smartened up to form an attractive pedestrian shopping area. Two blocks south is the Alfândega (see page 32) – the former Customs House, built in the 16th century and now converted to form the seat of the island's regional parliament.

The Old Town

Funchal's Zona Velha (Old Town) is a delightful area of the city where the tastes of well-heeled tourists are catered for in restaurants and night-clubs side by side with some of the poorest slums in the city. The area still has a gritty character but is rapidly being developed. *Allow 30 minutes.*

Start at the Praça da Autonomia.

1 PRAÇA DA AUTONOMIA

In the middle of the roundabout is the Autonomy Monument, celebrating the self-governing status Madeira achieved after the 1974 Carnation Revolution. The monument consists of a woman bursting forcefully out of her imprisonment in a block of bronze. This also marks the point where two of Funchal's canalised rivers meet and flow into the sea.

To reach the Old Town proper, you can either walk along the sea walls, or follow the café-lined street called Rua de Carlos I which runs parallel, to the north. In between is a plot of land which once served as the bus station, now a car park, where peasant farmers set up an extension of the Mercado dos Lavradores (Workers' Market) on Fridays.

2 LARGO DO CORPO SANTO

This narrow cobbled square gives you a good sense of the Zona Velha's contrasts. Cheek by jowl with numerous pavement cafés specialising in seafood is the shipyard, on the right, belonging to the Madeira Engineering Company where fishermen's trawlers are repaired. At the far end of the square is the little Capela do Corpo Santo, a simple chapel built by Funchal's fishermen in the 16th century. Beyond the chapel is the Fortaleza de São Tiago, built in 1614 as part of the city's defences. There are plans to turn the fort into a museum but for the moment it is locked and empty. To the right of the fort an alley leads through a small shanty town of shacks selling grilled fish to locals who come here to swim from the tiny pebbled beach, the Praia da Barreirinha. *Turn left by the fort up Rampa do Forte, then right to reach the church of Santa Maria Maior.*

3 IGREJA DE SANTA MARIA MAIOR

This church is situated in the poorest end of the Funchal but the area will, no doubt, become more prosperous once the new Lido swimming complex (under construction in 1994) opens to visitors. Santa Maria Maior church, opposite the Lido, is also known as the Igreja do Socorro (Church of Salvation) because the Apostle St James the Less, whose shrine is inside, helped to end a plague that hit the area in the 16th century. The present church is 18th century and has a theatrical air, with its painted ceiling, glass chandeliers and gilded pulpit, looking like an opera box. There are excellent views of the sea and of Funchal from the terrace in front of the church. *Turn right out of the church and follow Rua de Santa Maria all the way downhill.*

4 RUA DE SANTA MARIA

This street will take you past Arsenio's Fado Restaurant, a popular night spot where you can hear typical Portuguese fado music and song. As you approach the end of the road nearest to the Mercado dos Lavradores, or Workers' Market (see page 44) you will encounter all the bustle of shoppers, makeshift street stalls and hawkers selling everything from lottery tickets to bunches of garlic and herbs. *Turn right up busy Rua do Boa Viagem and you will soon come to the back entrance of the market where fishermen come to sell their catch. If the sight of ugly espada fish is not to your taste, turn left in Rua Latino Coelho and walk round to the front entrance where the market teems with people and stallholders selling colourful fruit, flowers and vegetables.*

Doorstep conversation in the cobbled pedestrian streets of the Old Town

São Vicente
Rabaçal
Pico do Arieiro
Ponta de São Lourenço
Quinta do Palheiro
Ribeira Brava
Funchal

Between the Rivers

The first part of this walk is for serious shoppers – there are lots of curious and interesting shops to dip into, muddled up in typically Madeiran style so that shops selling frivolous things like jewellery sit next door to shops selling useful things like tap washers or salted cod.

The walk then explores the area that lies between two of Funchal's rivers – both canalised as a precaution against autumn rains which can see the rivers rise from a trickle to 4m in depth. For the route, see the Central Funchal walk map on page 62. *Allow 30 minutes.*

Igreja do Carmo
(Carmelite Church)

Start in the street that runs northeast of Funchal's cathedral, the Rua do Aljube.

1 RUA DO ALJUBE

There is a good view up this broad street of the cathedral tower with its tile-covered spire, echoed by the tower of the Banco do Madeira, further up. On the left-hand side of the street Teixeiras (No. 15) sells fine embroidered blouses in modern styles and Maison Blanche (No. 19) is an up-market department store. Further up on the right costumed flowersellers have their stalls, shaded by bright umbrellas, and the street widens to form an attractive square. Here you will find the Bazar do Povo (Paupers' Bazaar) founded in 1883, a covered shopping mall where numerous retailers on three floors sell everything from table linen and carpets to religious statuary. This lines the whole north side of Rua do Betencourt which leads to the Ribeira de Santa Luzia. Crossing this river, ponder the fact that 600 people were killed in the floods that hit the city on 9 October 1803. As a consequence of that, the retaining walls you now see were built between 1804 and 1807 to contain this and the city's other two rivers, but there have been serious floods several times since, the most recent one on 29 October 1993.

Cross the river to busy Largo do Phelps. Shoppers may want to explore Rua Dr Fernão Ornelas, to the right, which also has interesting shops. Otherwise bear left to Carmo church.

Mock Moorish in Rua do Carmo

2 IGREJA DO CARMO

If you are lucky you may find the Carmelite Church open. Inside this 17th-century church are two very aristocratic tombs near the high altar, shaped like coffins resting on the backs of lions, and *azulejos* tiles depicting scenes from the life of Christ. If the church is closed, carry on up Rua do Carmo and you might have better luck visiting the embroidery showroom and factory called Madeira Superbia at Number 27 (first floor), next to the Cine Jardim and the Moorish-style building (now a laundry) at Number 33.

Retrace your steps up Rua do Carmo and turn right in Rua da Conceição.

3 RUA DA CONCEIÇÃO

This narrow lane has some of Funchal's oldest buildings, some in a poor state. Number 27, for example, is a fine Manueline building beneath the peeling façade, 17th-century in date and well worth restoring. Already restored are Numbers 49–53 with an ornate balcony, central tower and deep roof eaves. Further up at Number 71 you may be lucky (if it is a weekday) to see the blacksmith at work in his forge. Rua da Conceição continues the other side of Rua do Bom Jesus; it is worth continuing up a short way, if only to see Number 82, on the right, an embroidery warehouse with tiled façade, cast-iron balconies and an art deco door made for a giant!

Back on Rua do Bom Jesus turn right (east) past the 17th-century Bom Jesus church and across the river again. As you cross the river look right to see the former residence of Henry Veitch, who was British Consul from 1809 to 1836. Veitch designed the towered house himself and it is now occupied by the Madeira Wine Institute.

4 PRAÇA DO MUNICÍPIO

On the other side of the river you will pass the rather ugly Palácio da Justiça (Law Courts) on the right with a pollution-stained statue of Justice in front, and then the more attractive main square, the Praça do Município. To the east is the Câmara Municipal (see page 52), to the south the Bishop's Palace containing the Museu de Arte Sacra (see page 45) and to the north, with its façade covered in ecstatic saints, is the Jesuit Colégio Church (see page 36). To the west is the Bar O Leque, a good spot for coffee, shaded by a huge cucumber tree (*Kigelia africana*).

Once refreshed you might like to continue on to the Elegant Mansions walk, page 68–9.

São
Vicente

Rabaçal   *Pico do*   Ponta de São
           Arieiro   Lourenço

                    Quinta do
                    Palheiro
Ribeira
Brava   Funchal

Elegant Mansions

As the title of this walk indicates, the main
purpose of the route is to track down the best of
Madeira's ornate town houses, but with plenty of
other distractions along the way. For the route,
see the 'To the Waterfront' walk map on page 60.
*Allow 30 minutes for the walk – half a day or
more if you visit all the churches and museums
along the route.*

*Start in Praça do Município and walk east out of the square, along
Rua C Pestana. Cross Avenida Zarco into Rua da Carreira.*

1 RUA DA CARREIRA

This is one of Funchal's most interesting streets, lined with
ornate buildings. The predominant colours are white, grey and
green – olive green for the pretty wrought-iron balconies and

Delicate patterns
wrought from iron

the louvred shutters designed to exclude the searing sun, grey
for the carved stone door and window surrounds and white for
the plastered house façades. Most of the owners keep to this

colour scheme, but the effect is far from
monotonous because every building is
different and some have exuberant
displays of plants on their balconies.

Three doors up on the left is the
Pátio complex and Museu Photographia
Vicentes (see pages 52–3) with the
English Bookshop on either side of the
entrance gates and an open-air café in
the courtyard, shaded by fig and banana
trees. Further up on the left, at Number
75, is a baker's shop noted for its *bolo de
mel*, the so-called honey cake, black and
dense with nuts and fruit, but actually
made with molasses rather than honey.
Number 83 has an ancient shop sign
declaring itself to be the *Rei das
Mobílias* – King of the Furnishers; it sells
antique and reproduction furniture.
Opposite, Number 102 has a good
selection of wickerwork including
baskets, chairs and tables.

Take a look up Rua do Sardo, the

next right, which has many more ornate houses. Number 7, on the left, is one of the most plant-filled balconies on the island, a veritable cascade of ferns, geraniums and jade-green succulents.

Back on Rua da Carreira, Number 155 (the local army recruiting office) on the left, is one of the best buildings on the street, with long balconies on both upper floors made of wrought iron in a delicate fan-shaped pattern.

At the next right, Rua do Mouraria, look up to see Numbers 3–5, its windows gaily garlanded with floral motifs, somewhat out of keeping with its use as a funeral parlour.

At the next right, you can turn up Rua do Quebra Costas to see the English Church at Number 18, built in the early 19th century and set in a pretty garden (see page 36).

Continuing up Rua da Carreira you will finally reach the iron gates of the British Cemetery (ring for entry) with its moving memorials set in a tranquil bird-filled garden (see also page 36). Coming out of the cemetery, turn left, then right into Rua das Cruzes.

2 RUA DAS CRUZES

Towering above you is the Castelo de São João de Pico, the Peak Fort, built between 1580 and 1640 when Madeira (as well as all Portugal) was ruled by Spain. The massive fort is now used by the Portuguese Admiralty as a radio station, and so is closed to the public.
Follow Rua das Cruzes round to the right – you will pass a dull apartment block on the left, then a dignified house on the right that serves as the headquarters of Madeira's Ministry of Forestry, Agriculture and Fisheries. Bear right where the road divides to avoid the traffic, then climb the steps to the left and walk up to the terrace shaded by

Far-reaching views open up as you reach the end of this walk

a huge Indian fig tree (Ficus benjamina). From here there are good views over the English Church and out to the sea. Continue on beneath the walls of the Quinta das Cruzes, the lovely 17th-century villa and garden built on the site where Zarco, Madeira's discoverer, had his house (see page 54). Turn right here, down Calçada Santa Clara.

3 CALÇADA SANTA CLARA

Santa Clara church (see page 32) is where Zarco, the island's founder, is buried. From here continue down the steep road past the Museu Frederico de Freitas, another fascinating and elegant house open to the public (see page 51). At the bottom of the hill you will reach São Pedro church. The main attraction of this church, built in 1598 and remodelled in 1748, is the gilded altar surround and the ceiling painted with flowers, including roses, day lilies, Turk's cap lilies and chrysanthemums. To the right of São Pedro, in Rua do Mouraria, is the Museu Municipal (see page 52). *Opposite São Pedro, Rua das Pretas will take you back to the start point of the walk.*

TOWN HOUSES

Central Funchal has many fine town houses, most of them built during the 19th century. The grandest are known as *quintas*, roughly translated as 'mansion' or 'manor house'. Rural *quintas* are usually set in extensive grounds and are connected with some form of agriculture, such as wine production. In the town, *quinta* was simply the name given to the residence of a wealthy or prominent citizen. The dominant architectural style is baroque but a very restrained version of this often theatrical style. Door and window surrounds are usually carved into curvaceous shapes but the black-grey basalt used as building stone is too hard for elaborate moulding. Instead the city's architects achieved their impact through colour, contrasting the soft black of the window and door frames with the gleaming white of the rendered walls into which they are set. Wrought-iron balconies running the full length of the house provide the ornament for smaller houses, many of which are built around a plant-filled patio – such as the one to be seen at the Museu Photographia Vicentes (see page 52–3). Balconies, window shutters, gates and doors are traditionally painted green and the roofs are covered in terracotta tiles, so that looking down on the city from above, or approaching by ship, you will see landmark buildings, such as the cathedral tower, pointing a white finger above a sea of warm red. Legislation was passed in 1986 requiring owners to stick to these time-honoured colours, hence the pleasing harmony of the buildings in central Funchal.

Sunlight and shadow adds to the delightful variety of Funchal's architecture

Gardens and Levadas

This walk is designed to provide an introduction to the delights of walking along Madeira's unique irrigation canals, or *levadas* (see pages 136 and 138). It also provides you with a route between the two best gardens on Madeira. *The walk itself will take about 1.5 hours but allow a whole day if you want to spend time in the gardens, perhaps enjoying a leisurely picnic along the route.*

The walk is manageable by anyone who is reasonably fit and there are no steep drops to worry vertigo sufferers. The path can be muddy for several days after rain, so take walking shoes with a good grip.

1 QUINTA DO PALHEIRO
The walk begins at the Quinta do Palheiro (formerly known as Blandy's Gardens), located 8km northeast of Funchal and reached by bus 37 or taxi. The garden is only open mornings

Monday to Friday (see page 104) so you need to start out reasonably early if you want to explore the gardens fully.

2 LEVADA DOS TORNOS

This *levada* will take you to the Jardim Botanico (Botanical Garden). To reach the *levada*, turn right out of the Quinta do Palheiro gates, following the straight road that runs alongside the *quinta* wall. At the top of the hill (after 400m) you will come to a junction with a couple of cafés. Turn left and walk up past some smelly rubbish tips and rusting cars. At the crest of the slope turn left to follow the side wall of the white Ramazotti warehouse, with the sports stadium high up on your right. You will find the start of the *levada* at the back of the warehouse.

Following the *levada* footpath you will come almost immediately to a viewpoint on the left, located on top of the flat roof of the local school.

3 VIEWPOINT

The *levada* path passes through a mimosa wood and shortly afterwards meets the EN102 road – a spot whose scruffiness is rescued by the sweeping view over Funchal. This is an urban *levada* and some early stretches of the walk have rather more litter, traffic noise and barking dogs than you would normally want to encounter – it does, however, get much better soon. Cross the road and continue on the *levada* path through pine and mimosa woods, with views to the left of the Quinta do Palheiro and of the adjacent golf course. Continue for 1km until you meet the EN201 road.

4 TO THE QUINTA DO POMAR

After crossing the EN201 you will come to the most enchanting part of the walk as the *levada* twists and turns through a menthol-scented eucalyptus wood, heading up a narrow valley to maintain the same contour and back along the other side.

You are now well away from roads and the woods are silent except for the sound of running water and the song of birds. Enjoy this idyll while it lasts for you will return to 'civilisation' after 15 minutes' walking. Cross the tarmac road and walk past a *levada* station where the flow of the waters is controlled. Shortly after you will reach the Quinta do Pomar; there is no *levada* path here, so take the cobbled track on the right, then immediately left, going behind the *quinta* and its little neo-Gothic chapel. Return to the *levada* path and out, through a red iron door in the *quinta's* garden wall. From here, it is a steep 15-minute walk down to the Botanical Garden. You can, if you prefer to walk on the level, cross the road and continue along the *levada* path for another 15 minutes to the village of Romeiros; here you can catch bus 29 which passes the Botanical Garden on its way to Funchal.

5 JARDIM BOTÂNICO

If you choose to walk to the Botanical Garden from here, turn left and follow the steep cobbled road downhill. Where the main road swings left, after 4 minutes, carry straight on down the stepped cobbled path for a bird's-eye view of Funchal. At the next junction, the Restaurante Miranda on the right offers the chance to break for coffee. Turn right here, then first left down Caminho dos Voltas. After 10 minutes this leads to the Botanical Garden entrance (see page 40). There are taxis here for the return trip to Funchal, or you can take buses 29, 30 or 31.

TERRACES AND CROPS

The island of Madeira is a human artefact, shaped and sculpted by African slaves until slavery was abolished in 1775, and then by hardworking islanders engaged in backbreaking toil. Tumultuous geological forces formed the island's deep ravines and hidden valleys but human hands moulded the slopes into stepped terraces, piling up boulders to create retaining walls. Baskets laden with red-brown soil were carried up from the valley bottom – returning the soil that had been eroded by floods and rain after the early settlers had burned down the tree cover. Little by little the shape of the island was subtly changed, especially on the sunny southern side where the rocks and cliffs absorb sun by day, giving out warmth at night like a radiator. Here, from sea level up to 300m every patch of cultivable land is used to grow bananas, exported in quantity to mainland Portugal, grapes for wine and for eating, and exotic fruits such as mangoes, avocados, passion fruits and papayas. Higher up, market gardeners produce cabbages, carrots, onions, potatoes and yams in tiny fields interspersed by

Madeiran terracing, a monument to human perseverance

orchards devoted to citrus fruits, custard apples and figs. Higher still, at 400 to 700m, it is common to see fruit trees, such as apples, pears,

The fruits of
year-long
toil

plums and cherries, a delightful
sight when in blossom in
spring. The fruits are used to
make *ginja* (cherry liqueur),
sidra (cider) and other
warming distillations, as well
as being sold in Funchal's
market. Few edible crops are
grown above 700m in the
woodland zone and this is the point at
which the terracing usually stops; even
so, good use is made of the fertile
volcanic soil for growing eucalyptus,

the island's most important
timber crop, willows for weaving, and
bay trees for flavouring beef *espetada*.

Madeira's appearance changes constantly with the weather

EXCURSIONS

BOCA DA ENCUMEADA

The Encumeada Pass is famous for its views, but it really is pot luck whether the views will be of clouds or of deep green valleys at the time of your visit. The altitude of the pass is 1,007m, and the clouds tend to hang at the 800m level, so you may be bathed in sunshine even if the view below is obscured. On a clear day you can see the sparkling blue seas of the south coast and then by turning round 180 degrees, the wilder grey seas of the north. To the west is the flat top of the Paúl da Serra plateau and to the east are the great peaks and ridges of the central mountain range. The steep-sided valleys that lead up to the pass from the south and the north are lush, green and intensively cultivated. Together they form a deep cleft that seems almost to cut the island in two. If you want to linger for a while, try following one of the *levadas* that radiate out from the pass. The best is the Levada das Rabaças which starts opposite (south of) the restaurant and bar. Wild flowers abound on the first part of the route and there are splendid views to the south. You can continue for 15 minutes or so, to the point where the *levada* divides (the right-hand branch goes into a tunnel with a door). Beyond this point there is less to see; the hillsides have yet to recover from the destructive forest fires of the early 1990s.

Location: On the 104 road, midway between Ribeira Brava and São Vincente, 43km northwest of Funchal.

CABO GIRÃO

Cabo Girão is one of the most heavily promoted sights on Madeira, billed as the second highest sea cliff in Europe and one of the highest in the world. Guides tend to be rather vague if you ask which is Europe's highest cliff. Pedantic questions are silenced by the truly impressive views down an almost sheer drop to the Atlantic, 580m below. The name of the headland means 'Cape of the Turning', not because the view makes your head spin round, but because Zarco sailed this far on his first exploratory trip to Madeira before turning back to

Funchal, where he put down his anchor and decided to land. Those who can bear to look down the cliff face for very long will notice that there are tiny terraces dug into the face. It scarcely seems credible that anyone would dare cultivate such tiny and vertiginous plots, and yet the warmth of the south-facing cliffs has tempted some brave farmers to plant vines, flowers and vegetables.
Location: on the south coast, 22km west of Funchal.

CALHETA

Bathed in sunshine, Calheta is the main village of a sprawling district that thrives on horticulture; its houses with their pretty gardens seem lost in a sea of bananas and vines. Steep cobbled streets lead down to the coast and several of the region's churches have 16th-century features; they include the Chapel of Our Lady of Loreto, on the western outskirts of Arco da Calheta, Calheta's own church, which has a fine wooden ceiling,

The ubiquitous banana (below) and looking up to Cabo Girão (right)

and the Reis Magos Chapel at Estreito da Calheta. One of the most colourful festivals on the island takes place here on 7 and 8 September, when celebrations for the grape harvest and for Our Lady of Loreto become the excuse for decorating the streets with flowers, setting off noisy fireworks and enjoying beef *espetadas*.
Location: on the south coast, 62km west of Funchal.

Standard church opening times are 8am–1pm and 4pm–7pm but these can be subject to local variation.

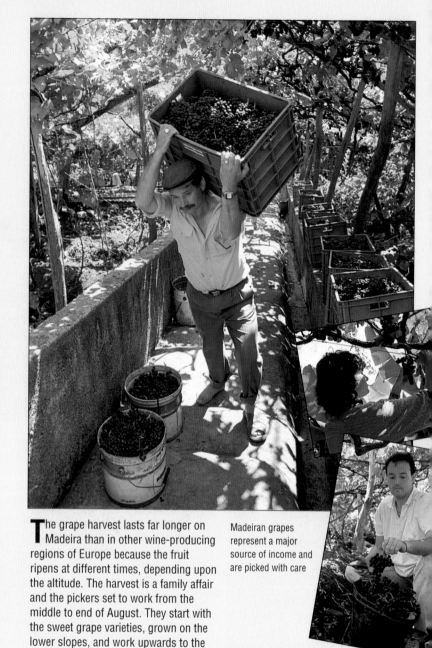

The grape harvest lasts far longer on Madeira than in other wine-producing regions of Europe because the fruit ripens at different times, depending upon the altitude. The harvest is a family affair and the pickers set to work from the middle to end of August. They start with the sweet grape varieties, grown on the lower slopes, and work upwards to the

Madeiran grapes represent a major source of income and are picked with care

THE GRAPE HARVEST

sercial vines, grown for the driest wines, at around 700m. They then return to sea level to end the harvest in early November, picking the muscatel grapes whose sugars have now been concentrated by the sun. If you are travelling round Madeira in the autumn it is difficult to miss the trucks laden with grapes bound for the factories of Madeira's leading wine producers; local people cannot wait the 20 years or so that it takes to produce fine Madeira, though, and a certain amount of the harvest goes into the production of fruity wines for purely local consumption, such as *canina* (from Estreito de Câmara de Lobos), *jaquet* (from Seixal and Porto Moniz) and *americana* (from Porto da Cruz). A little of this wine is still produced the traditional way, for old times' sake, by treading the grapes in a stone or cement tank called a *lagar*. Most of the grapes, however, are put through a stainless steel electric-powered press. The juice is placed in barrels and left to ferment – local wine is drunk very young and the first batch will be ready for tasting in early November, coinciding with the end of the harvest. Now everyone can relax and enjoy the fruits of their labour. Visitors to Madeira can enjoy the fruits without the hard work – Funchal hosts a month-long wine festival in September which is good fun, even if it is put on *para o inglês ver* (literally 'for the eyes of the English', i.e. for the benefit of tourists). For a taste of the real thing, head for

After the toil, enjoy the fruits

Estreito de Câmara de Lobos, 20km west of Funchal, the island's vineyard capital – here you can watch the harvest and take your pick from a number of bars and restaurants serving the local wines.

CAMACHA

Camacha is a village devoted to the production and sale of wickerwork. Almost everyone who lives here is employed in the industry, either as weavers or as vendors. The main building on the village square is the Café Relogio (Clock Café), a multi-storey emporium crammed with wickerwork and often crowded with coach-borne shoppers. Here you can see a vast range of wickerwork products, from tea trays, plant-pot holders and magazine racks, to peacock-backed chairs, bedheads and picture frames – enough, in fact, to furnish every part of the house if you were so minded. Most visitors content themselves with modest purchases – a shopping basket or gardener's trug, for example, which are easier to carry home by air. The shop will arrange freight forwarding for larger items if you wish, but the prices can be steep for bulky items. If you are lucky, you will be able to watch willow weavers at work in the supermarket basement. They work with extraordinary speed, the result of years of practice. Most weavers specialise in one

type of wickerwork – be it linen baskets or babies' cradles – and build up a proficiency over time. Just for fun, and to show off their artistic skills, a group of local weavers created a vast galleon, with billowing sails, and a Noah's Ark, with elephants, lions, monkeys and deer, displayed on the middle floor. None of these are for sale, a fact which disappoints some visitors. The Café Relogio (Largo Achada, tel: 922114) above the wicker warehouse is the venue for folk nights every Saturday evening when the local dance group, one of the best on the island, gives a spirited performance.

Location: 15km northeast of Funchal.

CÂMARA DE LOBOS

Sir Winston Churchill, the British wartime Prime Minister, is regarded with almost saintly reverence on Madeira because he helped to put the island on the tourist map. From 1949 he made regular visits to paint the local landscape, and in particular the little fishing village of Câmara de Lobos. Now a plaque on the wall alongside the busy 101 road east of the harbour marks the spot where Churchill sat to paint the view and local shops sell rather fuzzy black and white postcards of the great man at work, unmistakable with his trademark cigar and panama hat. It is interesting to speculate how much the fishing village has changed since Churchill's day. It looks as pretty as ever, with gaily painted boats drawn up on the tiny pebble beach. The tiny harbourside houses are painted in the same bright colours – primary red, yellow, blue and green against brilliant white. Yet there is an air of distressing poverty about the place as well – this is about the only village on Madeira where you are likely to be pestered by begging

Discussing the catch at the fishing village of Câmara de Lobos

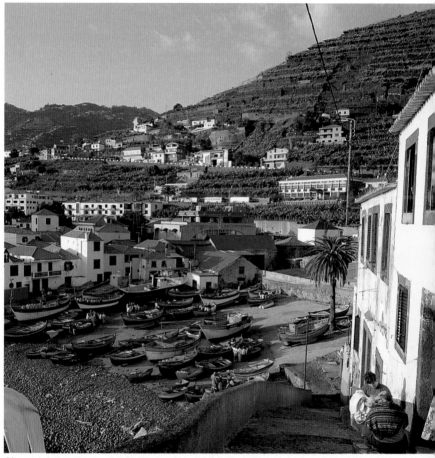

Câmara de Lobos: the view that Sir Winston Churchill loved to paint

children, and the streets running down to the harbour smell of more than just the detritus of the fishing industry. The fishermen here work all night to catch *espada* fish which are then sold in the harbourside wholesale market. You will have to come very early to see this in operation, since most of the trading is over by 7am. The busiest place in the village then becomes the nearby bar where the profits from a hard night's work can be easily gambled and drunk away. A tiny chapel in the bar district hints at the hardships of the fishing life: scenes from the life of St Nicholas, patron saint of seafarers, include vivid depictions of shipwrecks and drownings. *Location: 15km west of Funchal.*

WICKERWORK

Wickerwork is one of Madeira's most important cottage industries, employing some 2,500 people. The industry dates back to the 19th century when cane furniture was very popular and Madeirans began copying examples imported to the island by British visitors. Today the wicker products sold as souvenirs only represent a fraction of the island's total output, most of which is exported to the US and Europe.

Willows are grown all over the island at heights of 700 to 800m, where the cloud tends to hang, providing plenty of moisture. The trees are pollarded by having all their branches cut off at a relatively young age. This encourages the tree to produce lots of new shoots which can grow up to 2m in length in a single growing season. The shoots are harvested in January to March and left to soak in water before the bark is peeled off. They are then dried, often by being exposed to the sun on the roofs of willow weavers' houses. Before being woven into baskets or furniture, the canes are boiled to make them supple, which turns their colour from white to the more familiar brown. Walking around the countryside, you may well see great bundles of willow stacked in the sun, and you may even see weavers at work, seated on low stools outside their houses. Demonstrations of willow weaving can be seen at Camacha (page 80), the centre of the industry, where you can also marvel at the bewildering array of different wicker products – from simple placemats to the most ornate birdcages.

Willow weavers display their dexterity and skill

Caniço's church, an architectural masterpiece in grey and white

CANIÇAL

Caniçal is a gritty little working port where the fishing community gets on with its business as if the tourists were invisible. Most visitors come here for the Museu da Baleia (Whale Museum) but then find themselves drawn to the nearby beach where it is possible to stand around for an hour or more, watching the boat builders at work or the tuna fishermen bringing in their catch. It takes less time to view the museum itself, which contains an endearingly jumbled exhibition on the theme of the whale – sculptures, old engravings, ancient and modern scrimshaws carved from whale ivory, a lifesize wax model of a sperm

whale, 12m long, and a whaling boat of similar length. What is not immediately apparent is that this museum is conservationist in outlook – you have to watch the museum video to realise this. The rather slow-moving 45-minute documentary reveals how marine conservationists are tapping into the memories and experiences of retired Madeiran whale fishermen, many of them based in Caniçal, in order to understand more about the movements and habits of the sperm whale. Their comments, along with readings from Herman Melville's whaling classic, *Moby Dick* (1851), provide an informative commentary to the film itself, which shows scientists tracking a school of whales in the seas between Madeira and the Azores, filming them at play, feeding and even reproducing. The video shows that very little is known about these endangered whales and their movements, yet it is hoped that they will find a sanctuary off the coast of Madeira in the

Tuna fishing boats beached at Caniçal

newly established marine reserves (see page 130).

To the east of Caniçal you can see the building that once served as Madeira's principal whaling station, where whale carcasses were reduced to ivory, oil and

S². CORAÇÃO DE JESUS

complex, noted for its diving facilities: there is good diving off the beach here and at the nearby underwater nature park, 4km west at Ponta do Garajau. Literally translated, Ponta do Garajau means 'Tern Point' – so named because early explorers found a large colony of terns nesting on the cliffs below. Today its most prominent feature is a statue of Christ with outstretched arms, smaller than similar statues in Rio de Janeiro and Lisbon and erected in 1927. The headland commands good views to Funchal and the sunset can be dazzlingly colourful. If you decide that you want to linger on you can eat back in Caniço, where there is a good choice of several popular restaurants and bars catering to locals and to the German visitors who favour the nearby resorts.
Location: 9km east of Funchal.

The sailors' friend: images of the Redeemer (left and below) on the coast at Ponta do Garajau

ambergris (the waxy lining of the whales intestines, used in perfume manufacture). Now the building is part of the much bigger free port (Zona Franca) complex, intended to attract overseas investment funds and manufacturing to Madeira.
Location: 32km east of Funchal. Museu da Baleia open: Tuesday to Sunday, 10am–6pm.

CANIÇO

Caniço is worth a brief visit for its imposing 18th-century baroque church, whose tall belltower is visible to all motorists as they speed along the road from Funchal to the airport.

Some 2km southeast, on the coast at Caniço de Baixa, is the Roca Mar resort

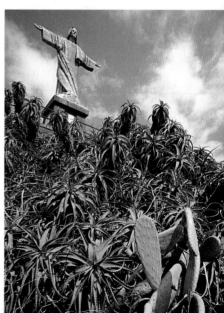

Curral das Freiras

Curral das Freiras means Nuns' Refuge, or Valley of the Nuns. The name derives from the fact that the nuns of Santa Clara convent (see page 32) fled here in 1566 to escape from pirates who were attacking the city. The green and unspoilt valley retains a sense of remoteness and otherworldliness today, despite the number of visitors who come here. It takes half a day to make the excursion, which illustrates how the mountainous terrain of Madeira can magnify distances.

The best route out of Funchal is to head westwards along the Estrada Monumental (101 road), passing through the Hotel Zone, then heading north on the 105. The first part of the journey is not very promising, as the road winds through the western suburbs of Funchal, past untidy housing estates, an army base and the clusters of satellite dishes used by the island's telecommunications authority.

São Martinho
Stopping off at São Martinho, you can take in the fine views from the terrace in front of the massive modern church (built 1930–52). Inside, in a room to the right of the main altar, is a small museum which doubles as a Sunday school. The exhibits include a silver processional cross and 18th-century garments, embroidered in gold, made for dressing up the religious statues on special feast days.

Pico dos Barcelos
From São Martinho northwards the views improve as you climb to this second viewpoint, located at 364m; several restaurants with terraces have been built here to take advantage of the views back to Funchal. Beyond this peak, take the 107 road (marked on some maps as the 203), following the narrow

winding road to Curral das Freiras as it climbs to the eastern side of the Socorridos valley, passing through eucalyptus woods.

Eira do Serrado
Before descending to Curral das Freiras, it is worth diverting to this 'eagle's nest' or eyrie, to look down on the village which forms the end point of the journey. To reach the viewpoint you first have to walk through a scruffy car park where stallholders will try to sell you T-shirts or locally made *ginja* (cherry liqueur). Once through this barrage you follow a path through sweet chestnut woods which are alive with dancing butterflies when the trees are in flower. The view from the *miradouro* is breathtaking and it reveals why some guides describe the valley as a crater – from this position you get the impression of being on the edge of a great cauldron, completely surrounded by towering cliffs and jagged peaks. This natural amphitheatre magnifies the sounds so well that you can hear every dog bark and hen crow from the tiny village far down below.

Curral das Freiras
The final descent to the village follows a road that was not built until 1959 and which passes through several rock-cut

Locked away in its own secret valley, the Nuns' Refuge that became a thriving village

tunnels. The old footpath linking the village to the outside world still exists, wide and grassy, zigzagging down the hillside – you can see the start of the path on the left after you emerge from the first tunnel. Once in the village the traditional thing to do, especially if you have walked all the way, is take coffee and eat the local speciality, warm chestnut bread, in one of the bars on the narrow main square. The Nuns' Valley Restaurant is regarded as the best bar – perhaps because the owner makes and sells his own *licor de castanha*, a liqueur which tastes like chestnut-flavoured gin, which he sells by the bottle or glass. If you come here on a Sunday there will normally be a street market in full swing. If not, you can walk on down the main street to the bottom of the valley and enjoy the peace of this favoured spot, basking in the sunshine and surrounded by dramatic scenery.

Location: 20km north of Funchal.

Machico

*A*fter Funchal, Machico is Madeira's second largest town, with a population of 13,000. The town is divided by the River Machico and sits at the mouth of a fertile green valley, backed by mountains. The intensively cultivated terraces clinging to the valley side show that many local people make their living in agriculture, while there is a small boatyard and fishing harbour on the coast. With the building of the Atlantis and Dom Pedro hotels on the western side of the town Machico has begun to develop as a tourist resort.

Some say that Machico is named after Robert Machin (see page 12), the English sailor who was shipwrecked on Madeira with his companions before the island was officially claimed by Portugal. Zarco is said to have found Machin's grave, marked by a rough cross of cedarwood, when he first landed. Others say that Zarco was moved by homesickness to name the spot after his native town of Monchique on mainland Portugal. Once settlement of the island got under way, Zarco ruled the western part from Funchal and his fellow navigator, Tristão Vaz Teixeira was appointed Captain General of the eastern part, ruling from Machico.
Location: Machico is 24km northeast of Funchal.

Igreja Matriz
Teixeira's statue stands on the town's main square, in front of the Igreja Matriz, the parish church of Machico. Though less ornate than Funchal's cathedral, this church is of similar date, founded at the end of the 15th century under the patronage of King Manuel I of Portugal and with a handsome Gothic portal.

Cristo Chapel
Older still is the Cristo Chapel, built, according to tradition, on the site of

Robert Machin's grave soon after Zarco landed on this spot. Floods have frequently damaged the chapel, which has been rebuilt numerous times, most recently in 1957. Locals call it the Capela dos Milagres (Chapel of Miracles) after the miracle-working crucifix inside (its miraculous powers now rarely sought, since the chapel is often locked). The crucifix lived up to its reputation in 1803 when floods devastated the chapel, washing all its contents out to sea. Not long afterwards, an American sailor landed on Madeira bearing the cross – he had spotted the image floating on the waves and was eventually able to return it to the rebuilt chapel. The crucifix is carried round the town in a festive torchlight procession on the nights of 8 and 9 October.

Forte do Amparo and Pico do Facho
Not far from the chapel is the triangular Forte do Amparo, built in 1708 near the seafront to provide Machico with some measure of defence against pirate raids. So devastating were these raids that a constant lookout was kept from the hill to the north of the town, known as the Pico do Facho (Torch Peak). Warning bonfires or beacons were lit if danger threatened and this practice is remembered every year on the last Sunday in August when a huge bonfire is

lit to celebrate the Festa do Santissimo Sacramento (Feast of the Holy Sacrament). Pico do Facho is easy to reach by road from Machico: take the Caniçal road and turn left just before the entrance to the road tunnel. There are fine views from the summit, with Santa Catarina airport, 4km to the southwest, prominent in the foreground and the cliffs of Ponta do São Lourenço in the opposite direction.

Machico's fishing fleet stands ready for a long night at sea

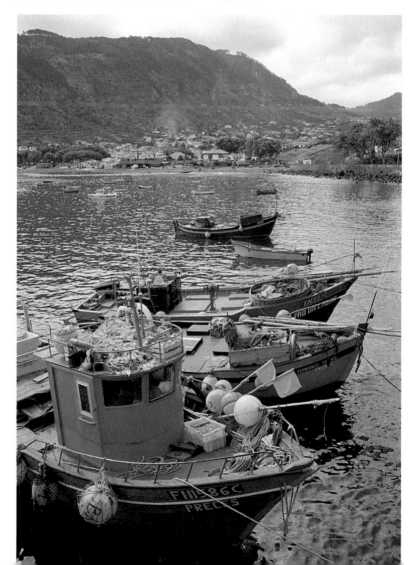

Monte

*T*he twin-towered church of Nossa Senhora do Monte is a prominent land-mark high on the hillside above Funchal. To devout Madeiran Catholics the church is a constant reminder of the Virgin's protective role as the island's patron saint. To visitors Monte means something quite different – the famous Monte toboggan ride which many consider to be the highlight of their trip.

Monte stands at 550m above sea level and the steep uphill journey used to be made by rack-and-pinion railway. This opened in 1893 and carried visitors from Funchal up the hillside, past the colourful gardens of numerous rural villas and mansions, to the station at Monte, taking 20 minutes to make the climb. Disaster struck in 1919 when one of the boilers of the steam locomotive exploded, killing four people and injuring many more. From then on, visitors and locals alike turned their back on the railway, regarding it as a dangerous means of transport. The company struggled on until 1939 when the railway was closed and the line dismantled.

Location: 6km north of Funchal. Monte Palace Tropical Gardens open: Monday to Friday, 9am–6pm. Admission charge. Monte church open: daily, 9.30am–1pm and 3pm–6pm.

Monte gardens

A short stretch of elevated viaduct survives from the old railway and this is the first sight that greets today's visitors arriving by car or bus. The station building survives on the shady main square, Largo do Fonte, as does the station garden, first laid out in 1894. The rather formal outlines of this garden have now been softened by the rampant green creepers that have cloaked the railway bridge in green and pushed out tendrils to spiral up the trunks of the tree ferns, obviously thriving in Monte's humid climate. A short way south of this public garden is the entrance to the Monte Palace Tropical Garden (Caminho do Monte 174), a relatively new arrival but one which promises to be the best on Madeira as it approaches maturity – the 7 hectares of hillside surrounding the Monte Palace have been skilfully planted with areas devoted to Madeiran flora, oriental species, azaleas, ferns and orchids.

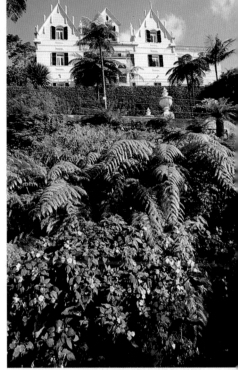

Already burgeoning: the recently created Monte Palace Tropical Garden

Nossa Senhora do Monte (Our Lady of Monte)

From the public gardens in Monte paths lead eastwards to the spot where white-suited toboggan drivers wait for passengers (see page 93), at the foot of the steps leading up to Monte church. Devout pilgrims who come to Monte for the island's major religious festival, the Feast of the Assumption on 15 August, will climb these basalt steps on their knees – there are 74 of them in total and it is a very steep climb, even on foot. The handsome church stands on the site of a chapel built in 1470 by Adam Gonçalves Ferreira who, with his twin sister Eve,

Pilgrims climb on their knees to visit Monte's revered church

was the first child born on Madeira. The church was rebuilt in baroque style following an earthquake and re-dedicated in 1818. Inside, in a silver tabernacle above the altar, is a precious statue of the Virgin which is carried in procession on the Feast of the Assumption. More imposing is the black coffin chest in the chapel to the left (north) of the nave which contains the mortal remains of the Emperor Charles I, the last in the long line of Hapsburg emperors. Crowned Emperor of Austria and King of Hungary in 1916, he was deposed in 1918 and exiled first to Switzerland and then, at his own request, to Madeira. He did not live long on the island, dying of a sudden attack of pneumonia in 1922, aged 35, leaving a wife and several children.

Terreiro da Luta

On the hillside just above Monte is the spot known as Terreiro da Luta, marked by a statue of the Virgin standing on top of a 5.5m-high column. It was in this spot that the little statue of the Virgin, revered in the church at Monte, appeared miraculously to a shepherd girl in the 15th century. The present statue dates to 1927 when it was erected in fulfilment of a vow made by devout Madeirans during the bombardment of Funchal by a German submarine in 1916. During World War I the Germans sought to end Madeira's use as a supply base for Atlantic shipping by sending in a submarine which first sank a number of ships moored in Funchal's harbour and then shelled the city itself. Appealing to the Virgin of Monte for protection, pilgrims promised to erect a statue in her honour. The bombardment ceased and Funchal survived the rest of the war unscathed, so grateful Madeirans created the present memorial. Round the foot of the monument is a symbolic rosary. This is made from the anchor chains salvaged from Allied ships sunk in the harbour by German torpedoes.

A short step away from the monument is the terminus of the defunct Funchal to Monte railway (see page 90). The palatial station building, which opened in 1912, also served as a restaurant. Today it continues to be used for receptions and functions. Passengers visiting Madeira on luxury cruise liners are often brought here for cocktails and to enjoy the expansive views down over the grey-green heads of fragrant eucalyptus trees to the red roofs of Funchal, some 876m below. It is then *de rigueur* to make the descent back to Funchal by toboggan, using a method of transport that has thrilled and intrigued visitors to Madeira for nearly 150 years. If you yourself do not want to make the trip, the toboggan drivers, dressed in traditional straw hat and white flannels, will usually let you take their photograph in return for a small tip.

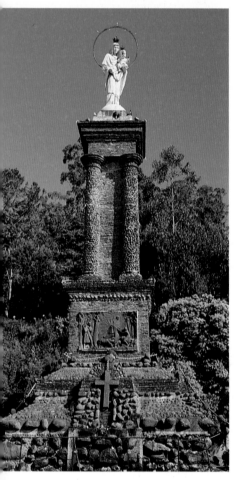

The Virgin of Monte, invoked to protect Funchal from war-time bombing

The Monte toboggan can reach surprising speeds

THE MONTE TOBOGGAN

Hemingway, not a man given to expressing strong emotions, described the toboggan ride from Monte to Funchal as one of the most exhilarating experiences of his life. Sliding in a wicker basket on wooden runners over the polished cobbles, toboggans can at times reach considerable speeds, though the drivers, with their rubber soled boots for grip, ensure that corners are negotiated safely. Sadly, the high cost of maintaining cobbled roads is encouraging the increased use of tarmac and the descent of the toboggans over certain sections of the run is becoming perceivably slower as a result.

Madeiran tobogganing, as a method of transport, was invented in 1850, it is said, though horse and bullock-drawn sleds were in use for transport well before that date. Some visitors consider this the essential Madeiran experience but it does not come cheap. You can go all the way to Funchal on a 4km ride, lasting 20 minutes, for around 2,200 *escudos* per person (two people per sled) or take the shorter run to Livramento (2km; 10 minutes) for 1,500 per person. You will, though, be expected to tip the drivers and pay for the rather blurred polaroid photograph that the driver's colleague will take along the route, expecting to sell it to you as a souvenir at the end of your brief journey.

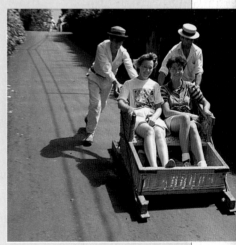

PAÚL DA SERRA

As if to prove that Madeira is not one vast floating flower garden the Paúl da Serra looms bleakly to the eastern end of the island. The name Paúl da Serra means Desert Plain, a very apt description for the high plateau where the soil is so thin that only the toughest of grasses will grow.

This is cropped tight by goats, sheep and sturdy little cows, their numbers strictly limited to prevent all the vegetation from being consumed. Travelling across the plain to Rabaçal or Porto Moniz, you will see caves dug into the sides of embankments to provide shelter for the farmers and for their beasts. You will also see their more modern, but substantially less-aesthetic, equivalent, large concrete sheds. Shelter is necessary because it is often very windy up on top of the plateau and this is where the snow will fall, if at all, during the winter months.

A forest of wind turbines has recently been built on the plateau to provide electricity to settlements along the island's north coast, the gleaming white towers and propeller blades looking very high tech and modern in contrast to the elemental moorland. It is not always wet, windy or misty up here, however, and in summer people come here to camp, play football in the big flat open spaces and look for the delicious fruits of the bilberry.

The Paúl da Serra also plays a vital role in the island's irrigation system. Rainwater is captured and channelled into reservoirs from which the water is fed into power stations and *levadas*. The

The unexpectedly flat expanse of moorland on Madeira's high plateau

volcanic rock of the Paúl da Serra also acts as a huge sponge absorbing rainfall which then filters down through the porous substrata until it meets layers of impermeable clay at around the 1,000m level. Here the water pours out of the ground, sometimes to cascade as spectacular waterfalls (at Rabaçal, for example; see page 121) but more often to feed the island's extensive *levada* network (see page 138).
Location: 60km northwest of Funchal.

PICO DO ARIEIRO

At 1,810m, this is Madeira's third highest mountain peak, and its most accessible (see page 124 for a walk). You can drive from the centre of Funchal to the top in little under an hour. Just before the peak, you will pass a small round-roofed ice house on the left, built in 1800 to store compressed snow which supplied Funchal's hotels with ice in the days before refrigeration. Snow is a relatively rare occurrence. Most of the time visitors bask in bright sunshine, high above the rainclouds, enjoying views that stretch across the whole of the island. Connoisseurs of the night sky and the dawn light say that you have not lived until you have spent a night on the mountain to view the Milky Way and the shooting stars that rain down in the early hours of the morning, followed by the most spectacular sunrise. Fortunately you do not have to rough it to spend a night on the mountain. The government-owned *pousada* (guesthouse and restaurant), just below the summit, provides every modern luxury.
Location: 23km north of Funchal.

PICO RUIVO

Just as spectacular is the sunrise viewed from Madeira's highest peak, the

Dawn above the clouds at Pico do Arieiro. Madeira's highest peaks are linked by knife-edge ridges and plunging cliffs

1,862m Pico Ruivo. Unfortunately, this mountain summit is much less accessible but you can walk to it along the well-marked path from its smaller neighbour, Pico do Arieiro (see page 124), provided that you have a head for heights and the time (allow 3 hours each way). Alternatively you can drive from Santana to Achada do Teixeira and walk the final stretch up the eastern flank of the mountain (allow 45 minutes each way). There are glorious views over the northeastern coast along the route and from the peak.
Location: 45km north of Funchal via Santana.

VOLCANIC ROCKS

Standing on the top of Pico do Arieiro, the view in every direction is of classic volcanic rock formations enough to send a geologist into paroxysms of excitement. Even to the non-specialist the parched sponge-like rocks in spectacular colours, such as purple, orange, chocolate and red, speak of tumultuous volcanic events. The central mountains of Madeira are made up of solidified lava and ash which began to form beneath the sea in the Miocene Era, 20 million years ago, gradually building up until the lava broke the water's surface, forming a small conical island. Further eruptions

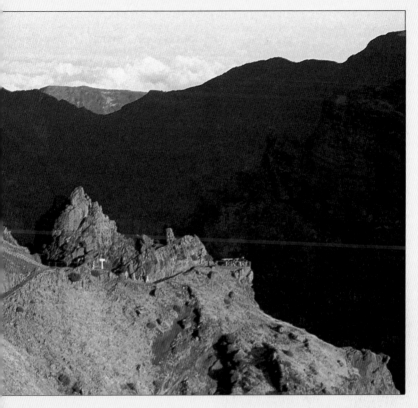

Dawn light enhances the colours of the rocks on Madeira's high peaks

then spilled lava down the eastern and western flanks, resulting in the present elongated shape. Massive earth movements also played a part, tilting, squeezing and crushing the layers of solid rock, so that you can see cliffs on Pico do Arieiro where different coloured strata are squashed and folded into bizarre concertina shapes. Hot lava continued to push through joints, gaps and weak points in the rock, so that you will also see great columns and beds of hard basalt interlayered with softer

tufas and compressed ash. When all the volcanic activity ceased, about 1.7 million years ago, weathering began – rain and river erosion created the island's spectacular ravines and knife-edge ridges, cutting deep into the weakest, softest rocks and leaving the hard rock still standing.

As a result Madeira now consists of a central spine, composed of lofty mountains, the remains of the original volcanic peaks, and numerous deep valleys running off to the north and south, lush with the dense vegetation that Madeira's climate and the fertile soil combine to support.

POISO

The pass at Poiso is a favourite stopping-off point for walkers and travellers exploring the high peaks of the island's interior because the Abrigo do Poiso restaurant on the crossroads is a welcoming place, with a log fire to comfort chilled or wet bodies. The same fire is used for grilling delicious beef *espetadas*. Poiso sits on the eastern edge of the Montado do Barreiro National Park, an area of woodland and open moors, threaded by a tortuously winding narrow road (only open 8am to 7pm). Experiments are being made here in reafforestation to give this part of Madeira back its original wooded outline

Fragrant eucalyptus, introduced from Australia as a source of timber

and produce commercially valuable timber. Maritime pine, eucalyptus (Tasmanian blue gum), Douglas fir, Lawson cypress, Japanese red cedar and Indian silver fir are the principal trees being planted. Wild ponies, wild boar and rabbits are found here – all said to be the descendants of animals imported by early settlers. Rabbits have become such a nuisance that hunting is allowed on Thursdays and Sundays in September, October and November – it is best not to wander off the beaten track on these occasions because of the danger of stray shot. Barbecue pits, spring-water taps and picnic tables are scattered around the park, and on summer weekends Madeirans love to come here to camp.

Small patches of natural Madeiran vegetation can be found within the remoter valleys of the park, a tiny fraction of the dense woodland that covered the island until it was burned and felled by the early colonisers. Madeirans call these patches of indigenous woodland the *lauri silva*, meaning laurel woods. The laurels concerned are the *Laurus azonica*, which is a type of bay tree, and the Canary laurel (*Apollonius barbajuna*), both tough low-growing evergreens with leathery leaves. These are usually found growing in association with the *til* tree (*Ocotea foetens*), whose flowers have a sharp penetrating scent, and the *vinhático* (*Persea indica*), used by the early settlers for furniture making and known as Madeiran mahogany for its colour and hardness.

Location: 10km north of Funchal

PONTA DELGADA

Ponta Delgada is a small village on the north coast noted for its tiny harbour and for its willow-tree plantations, providing

The red roofs of Ponta Delgada, sheltered by tree-clad hills

the raw material for the island's wickerwork industry. The best time to visit is on the first Sunday in September when the Feast of Senhor Jesus is celebrated and the whole village is decked out in festive flowers and greenery. The festival celebrates an ancient crucifix which was washed ashore here in the 16th century. Believing it to be miraculous, the local people built a chapel to house the crucifix but a fire destroyed the building and consumed most of the cross in 1908. Undeterred, the villages rebuilt the church and they still revere the charred cross fragments, which are displayed in a glass case for most of the year.

Location: 27km west of Santana on the north coast, 60km from Funchal.

PONTA DO PARGO

Ponta do Pargo, or Dolphin Point, is the westernmost headland on Madeira and you can walk out to the lighthouse at the tip for views of the coast, knowing that nothing lies beyond this point except Atlantic waves until America is reached. If you are interested in wild flowers, you should walk the Levada Nova, which runs from Ponta do Pargo to Calheta (a distance of 20km but the 101 road with frequent bus services to Funchal is never very far away if you get tired). The combination of moisture and sunshine ensures that the margins of this *levada* have some of the most varied and colourful flowers to be found on the island.

Location: 78km west of Funchal.

Massive cliffs mark the easternmost tip of Madeira at Ponta de São Lourenço

visible offshore to the southeast, are a continuation of the same basic geological formations, though separated by a drowned valley some 100m deep. For the romantically inclined this is a spot to savour for its wild and breezy loneliness (see page 128 for a suggested walk) but when that palls you can take a dip in the more protected Praínha Bay, signposted to the south of the 101 road, midway between Caniçal and the end of the road. The beach is reached by means of a steep path near the chapel of Nossa Senhora de Piedate. Though not large, this is the only beach on Madeira with sand – black sand composed of crushed shells in which you may find tiny fragments of vegetation fossilised by volcanic ash. *Location: 32km east of Funchal.*

PONTA DO SOL

Ponta do Sol basks in the sunshine after which it is named: Sun Point is the last village travelling westwards along Madeira's southern coast to receive day-long sunshine – beyond here, cliffs and hills cast shadows in the early part of the day, especially when the sun is low in winter. Exploiting the sunshine to full effect, Ponta do Sol is a major centre of banana cultivation, and there is very little space around the town not covered by plantations: even the cliff faces have tiny terraces hacked out of them supporting a few banana plants, as you will see if you follow the coast road – look out for steps cut in the rock face and precipitous paths leading to terraces as you approach the tunnel that leads to Madalena do Mar. The effort of creating and tending such terraces is justified by the extra warmth given out by the rock face at night,

PONTA DE SÃO LOURENÇO

The easternmost tip of Madeira does not dip gracefully down to the sea with gentle gradient; true to the tumultuous character of the island's terrain, it stops abruptly at the precipitous edge of several canyon-like cliffs, 180m or more above sea level. Atlantic waves pound the base of the cliffs, undermining them gradually so that every so often great rocks crash down to join the smashed up boulders already littered chaotically between the cliffs and the sea. If you could see beneath the waves you would discover that the Ilhas Desertas, usually storing sunlight by day and acting as a radiator. This helps to ripen the crop sooner in the year, and can mean a premium price if the bananas are ready for sale well before the main crop. Some 600,000kg of bananas are exported from Madeira every year, much of it to Lisbon for sale in mainland Portugal. Ponta do Sol has one of the island's principal packing stations, unmissable because of the stalks piled outside the warehouse beside the main road, waiting to be pulped and processed into animal fodder or glues.

The next-door village of **Madalena do Mar** has an interesting history, for tradition attributes the founding of the village to King Ladislav of Poland. Having been defeated at the Battle of Varna in 1414, Ladislav set off on a pilgrimage round the world, visiting holy sites and doing good wherever he could.

Even the cinema (left) in Ponta do Sol alludes to the sunshine after which the village is named.
Decorating the streets (above) in preparation for Madeira's June flower festival

His travels eventually brought him to Madeira, where Zarco, the island's discoverer, persuaded him to settle, granting him the land around Madalena do Mar. Knowing nothing of his history locals called him Henrique Alemão – Henry the German. It was he who founded Madalena do Mar's little church of Santa Catarina in 1457.
Location: 42km west of Funchal.

Porto Moniz

*P*orto Moniz is located at the remote northwestern tip of Madeira, about as far as you can get from Funchal, and not so long ago there were people in the village who had never seen the island's capital. Even today it feels different from other villages on Madeira, despite the fact that it has rapidly caught up with the modern world and now boasts several hotels, cafés and restaurants, and the island's only official campsite.

The recent arrival of roads and electricity has given a boost to the village, opening it up to tourism, but for many the slow pace of the old life continues. Few people are wealthy enough to own vehicles – walking, often with heavy burdens, is still the norm. Road embankments, built or patched up with concrete elsewhere, are masterpieces of drystone walling round here, and they support a rich flora, covered in succulent

Dried heather fences protect the tiny fields of Porto Moniz from sea winds

house leeks and other wall plants. The tiny fields are meticulously cultivated, as you will see if you look down on the village from above – there is a fine viewpoint to the north of the village on the 101 road. The terraces that tumble down the hillside and the flat fields round the village itself are all fenced with dried heather and bracken, creating a low boundary about 0.5m in height, sufficient to protect the crops from strong Atlantic winds, driving rain and salt-laden sea spray. Descending into the village you will find all the paraphernalia

Wild seas, sheer cliffs and cascading waterfalls mark the north coast road

of a developing seaside resort, including a go-kart track and shops selling buckets and spades, despite the absence of sand. This is all part of a general diversification scheme to help the villagers reduce their dependence on agriculture. For many visitors, Porto Moniz is the start or end point of a drive along the spectacular north coast road (see below) and it has several excellent restaurants serving seafood which attract coach parties at lunchtime. For those with longer to stay, there is an unusual swimming pool next to the Residencial Calhau hotel on the edge of the ocean. Here, natural rock pools in the volcanic rocks have been deepened and linked by concrete pathways – you cannot swim far in the pools, but you can bask in the sun-warmed water while watching the Atlantic waves rolling in and beating against the shore.

Location: 75km north west of Funchal.

North Coast Road

You will see more of these mighty waves as you drive the exhilarating north coast road from Porto Moniz to São Vicente (see page 114). The road is one of those spectacular pieces of construction in

which the Madeirans seem to excel – like the island's *levadas*, construction of the road was achieved by the slow manual process of hacking away at the stone to create a narrow ledge in the cliff side, sometimes passing through tunnels. No machinery or modern technology made the task easier, and that is why the road took 16 years to complete, almost one year for each kilometre of its 19km length. Drive slowly, because the road is only wide enough for one vehicle in places; keep an eye out for oncoming vehicles and be prepared to pull over into a passing place if necessary. While waiting you can admire the wild seas, the sheer cliffs and the numerous waterfalls which cascade over them, very often soaking your car or – as the Madeirans say – giving you a free car wash.

Quinta do Palheiro
(Blandy's Gardens)

*O*f all Madeira's gardens, this one is the most rewarding and by following the Gardens and Levadas walk (page 72) you can combine a morning spent here with a visit to Funchal's Jardim Botânico for a day of horticultural indulgence. The gardens were first laid out in the 18th century by the original owner, the wealthy Count of Carvalhal, but his heirs proved profligate with their inheritance and the estate was purchased from them by the Blandy family in 1885. Successive generations of the Blandy family have tended the garden with its interesting blend of English-style design and tropical planting.

If you arrive by car, you can drive from the ticket office at the entrance down to the car park by the house, but walkers will enjoy the stroll down the cobbled drive. Here trees interspersed with camellias and massed agapanthus line the avenue with a view to the left on to a scene that could almost be in England, of

hay meadows and woodland. This garden is located at 550m above sea level, so it is cool and moist enough for oak, beech and chestnut trees to thrive, planted by the Blandy family decades ago to remind them of their English origins. At the bottom of the drive, signposts direct you to a sunny terrace below the house hung with scented jasmine, roses and other climbers. In the beds below, butterflies dart about amid colourful salvias and verbenas. From the centre of the terrace there is a stone staircase, flanked by flame-shaped Italian cypress trees and terracotta urns, which gives a good view of the house (not open to the public). Below the staircase is a wide path lined with rare and unusual trees such as the sweet-scented magnolia-like *Michelia doltsopa* and the ancient gnarled *Hagerstromia indica*, a Chinese tree which sheds its bark to reveal fresh colours beneath. Midway down this central walk, a path to the left leads to a bridge across a frog-filled pond and to a little chapel, built in restrained baroque style by the Count of Carvalhal.

Beyond the chapel is a magnificent long border, modelled on a typical

Tropical plants add exotic interest to a garden that is essentially English in style

English herbaceous border, but planted with spectacular abutilons, angel's trumpet (*Datura sanguinea*) and other tender plants among the blue delphiniums and multi-coloured sweet peas.

The most beautiful part of the garden comes next: the Ladies' Garden is a lovely serene spot for sitting and basking in the warmth, enjoying the birdsong, while looking out over hedges clipped to the shape of numerous peahens sitting on their nests. The topiary forms are made from *Muelenbeckia*, an Australian plant similiar to box, that lends itself well to clipping into intricate designs. Among the striking plants here is a wonderfully gnarled *Saphora japonica* tree, fringed by a cascade of branches sweeping down from the crown of the tree to the ground, and a *Sparmannia africana* whose simple white flowers open to reveal wonderful yellow and scarlet stamens, much visited by bees.

A path to the right of this garden leads out through a low iron gate into a long alley of plane trees and up to the Count of Carvalhal's 18th-century house, fronted by giant holm oaks and three

Striking flower and foliage colours can be guaranteed year round on Madeira

deep water troughs which the local frogs have colonised. Beyond the house, an area of woodland eventually takes you back to the formal gardens. Look for a signpost pointing left to Inferno (Hell)! Far from being infernally hot, this wild area of cool wet shaded woodland is full of graceful tree ferns and masses of vivid blue trailing morning glory vine.

Location: 8km east of Funchal, off the 102 Camacha road. Open: Monday to Friday, 9.30am–12.30pm. Admission charge.

The unspoiled virgin vegetation of Rabaçal's hidden valley

RABAÇAL

Rabaçal itself consists of no more than a government resthouse but the surrounding woods are some of the most scenic on Madeira, a rich ecological community of ancient laurel and tree heath, rich in ferns, mosses and lichens as well as thistles, geraniums and foxgloves in season. Well watered by *levadas*, you can follow paths to the Risco waterfall or the beauty spot known as the *Vinte e Cinco Fontes* (25 Springs) a pool into which scores of little water courses either drip or pour, depending on the time of year and the amount of rainfall. (see the Risco Waterfall walk, page 120). *Location: 65km northwest of Funchal, on the Paúl da Serra road to Porto Moniz.*

RIBEIRA BRAVA

Ribeira Brava started out as a watering hole, the point along the island's southern coast where several roads and paths meet and a place where weary travellers would rest and refresh themselves before continuing with their journey. Old habits die hard and even in this era of swift motorised transport few Madeirans pass through the town without stopping for a cup of coffee and a rest, hence the more than usually large seafront parking area and the number of nearby bars. Here, too, is a small covered market, a miniature version of Funchal's Mercado dos Lavradores, where fish, flowers, fruit and vegetables are sold. The name of the village, Ribeira Brava, means Wild River. Most of the year you will search in vain for evidence that the river running to the west of the town deserves such a dramatic name, but heavy rains in autumn can see the water level rise to 3 or 4m, and the bed is strewn with boulders and debris brought down from the mountains by flash floods. The sea can be equally wild, hence the massive concrete breakwaters piled upon the pebble beach to absorb the force of the waves. It is unlikely that you would be tempted to swim here, but you may want to explore the little fishing harbour, to the east of the town, through an archway cut in the cliffs. In the grid of streets stretching north from the waterfront you will find several characterful shops and typical examples of Madeiran town architecture – houses with ornate balconies and green window shutters.

Ribeira Brava is the start point for some attractive *levada* walks leading up the valley to the Boca da Encumeada pass, and the town has two modern hotels that are popular with walkers. *Location: 32km west of Funchal.*

Characterful Ribeira Brava

São Bento (St Benedict)

On the main square, São Bento church is one of the most interesting on Madeira, with several features surviving from the original 16th-century building. One of these is the unusual painted stone font, carved with interlace, grapes, pomegranates, cable motifs and wild beasts, including wolves. Similar beasts are carved on the base of the wall pulpit and on the capitals of the arches nearest to the high altar. The original altar surround was moved to the left-hand aisle during modernisation work in 1948. It consists of a carved and gilded tabernacle and reredos with a Flemish painting of the *Nativity* above.

Much of the chancel, painted to resemble marble, is modern but there is a 16th-century wooden sculpture of the Virgin above the high altar.

RIBEIRO FRIO

Most tour buses stop at Ribeiro Frio on the way to Santana, hence the size of the souvenir shop that dominates this little forest resort where the principal attraction is a trout farm. Set in a pretty garden, this consists of several concrete tanks fed by the fresh waters of the Ribeiro Frio (literally 'Cold River') from which the place gets its name. There is a limit to how long anyone can sustain interest in the antics of thrashing rainbow trout, but if you have time to kill you can try exploring one of the nearby *levada* paths. These start just below the Ribeiro Frio's bar and restaurant and are signposted. To the right is the path to Portela: for experienced walkers, this

Turning trout, Ribeiro Frio

12km walk is well worth doing – it is considered one of the best walks on the island but it does involve negotiating rock-cut tunnels and steep drops.

Just about anybody could manage the first 15 minutes or so of the walk, however, which passes through an area of virgin laurel and heath woodland, typical of the vegetation which covered Madeira until clearance began in the 15th century. A little further down the road from the bar is another signpost to the left labelled Balcões (meaning 'Balconies'). After following this *levada* for 20 minutes you will reach the viewpoints to which the name refers, high above the valley of the Ribeira da Ametade. The panoramic views take in the high peaks of Madeira's central mountain range to the west, and the lumpy outline of Eagle Rock (Penha de Águia) on the northeast coast.
Location: 14km north of Funchal.

SANTA CRUZ

It is worth stopping at Santa Cruz even if the former tranquillity of this historic town has been sacrificed to the nearby airport and the busy 101 road. The church here, founded in 1533, is one of the least altered on the island, with its bulky belltower and cross-shaped battlements and Gothic interior. Two other buildings of note nearby are the town hall and courthouse, and there is a colourful market on the seafront.
Location: 17km northeast of Funchal.

SANTO DA SERRA

Santo da Serra occupies a low plateau to the east of Madeira. It has its own microclimate and is often under cloud, rain or mist when nearby Funchal is dry and sunny. Despite this, wealthy city merchants began to build mansions here from the 18th century and the area acquired a reputation as a healthy summer resort.

Today it is best known by sports-loving visitors as the location of a fine golf course (see page 159) with sea views from the fairways and pine plantations reminiscent of the Scottish Highlands. In the centre of the village is the entrance to an extensive public park (open daily during daylight hours) which locals know as the camellia garden, because of the numerous camellias planted along the main central avenue. The extensive gardens, which once belonged to the Blandy family, also feature tennis courts, a children's playground and some sad-looking deer, ponies, birds of prey and a kangaroo, kept within small enclosures. If you follow the main avenue downhill you will come to a viewpoint where you can look out to Ponta de São Lourenço and the easternmost tip of the island. *Location: 22km northeast of Funchal.*

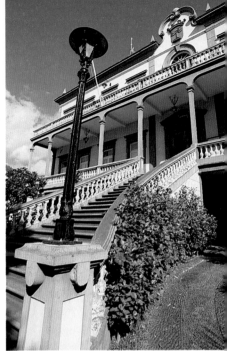

The courthouse (above) in Santa Cruz and one of Ribeiro Frio's *levada* paths (below)

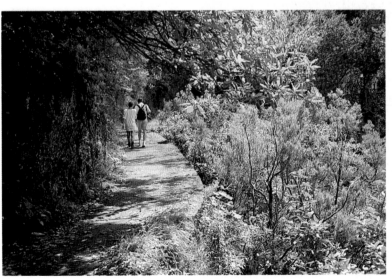

Santana

*T*he lush valleys around Santana are among the most beautiful and unspoiled on Madeira. By contrast with Funchal and the urbanised south of the island, Santana, the uncrowned capital of the north, is undeveloped, a place where traditional Madeiran life continues unaffected by the modern world and where the intensively cultivated and terraced landscape is like a cross between Bali and the Alps.

You will have plenty of opportunity to observe the local agriculture as you journey to Santana, passing fields where cabbages, carrots, potatoes, yams and maize are grown, yielding two or even three crops a year. The roadsides and every patch of uncultivated land are ablaze with the crimson of red hot poker (known as 'fire flowers' in Portuguese), agave, poinsettia, fuchsia, nasturtiums or monbretia, depending on the time of year.

Cutting and drying maize in Santana

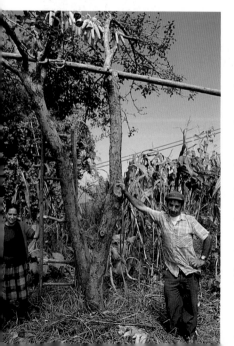

Thatched cowsheds (see page 112) dot the valley sides, and orchards provide apples, pears, plums, cherries, figs and mulberries. When you add to this the luscious fruits of blackberries, loganberries, strawberries and grapes, all grown locally, you will understand why the people of the region are nearly self-sufficient in food.

Santana itself is famous for its A-framed houses (see page 112). Right in the centre of the village is a house of this type open to visitors, inevitably part of a souvenir shop and restaurant complex, but none the less worth a look, since it is authentically furnished and will give you an idea of how comfortable these houses can be. You will see plenty of authentic examples as you wander round the village lanes – genuine lived-in houses set in impeccable gardens. These houses are often interspersed with tiny fields where barley and wheat are grown before being cropped by hand – partly for flour and animal feed, but also for thatching straw to keep the roofs repaired.

Santana is a good place to stop for lunch, since the main restaurant, the O Colmo, serves good locally produced food, including fresh trout from the farm at Ribeiro Frio (page 108) and delicious goat's cheese with honey.

Nearby
From Santana you can take the inland

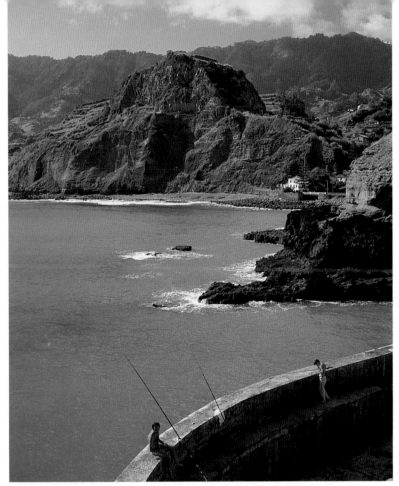
Porto da Cruz, once a bustling little port, now a peaceful and scenic backwater

road southwards to **Queimadas**, the start point for several spectacular *levada* walks, including the one that goes to the well-named **Caldeirão do Inferno** (Hell's Cauldron); you can also continue to the end of the same road and walk up to the top of Madeira's highest peak, **Pico Ruivo** (see page 95).

On the journey back from Santana, the view is dominated by the flat-topped **Penha de Águia** (Eagle Rock), a mountain-sized rocky outcrop separating **Faial** and **Porto da Cruz**. These two villages are typical of the little port towns that thrived in the era before motorised transport when boats were used to carry goods around. Porto da Cruz is a well-preserved example, with its ancient Roman-tiled houses and its stone-built harbour. Few boats use it now, but the local children come here to dive and swim in the deep clean water, sheltered from the force of the Atlantic waves.

What is the difference between a cowshed and a traditional Madeiran *palheiros*, or A-framed house? You may ponder this question as you wander round Santana because in both cases the construction is identical: both have a triangular façade with a thatched roof sweeping from the gable ridge right down to the ground. One answer is that houses usually have pots of trailing geraniums by the door and the façades are often boldly painted in crimson, white, yellow and blue. The other answer is, of course, that one has human occupants while the other is inhabited by a cow. Cows in this part of Madeira cannot be left to roam – they would break their legs on the steep slopes, damage the terraces and destroy crops. For their own safety they are kept in a triangular byre, whose thatched roof keeps them warm in winter and cool in summer.

They are milked daily and well looked after; you may see their owners climbing the hillside beneath a vast pile of grasses and hay with which they are fed. There is a surprising amount

COWSHEDS & PALHEIROS

of room inside, just as there is inside a *palheiros*, the human version – this usually has an upper storey, reached by a ladder, for sleeping and storage – separate toilets are placed away from the house and meals are prepared out of doors to avoid the risk of fire and prevent the cottage being filled with smoke and cooking smells.

Sometimes you will see sad examples of neglected cottages where the owner has died or moved away. Without constant loving attention the

houses soon decline, and the thatch is then replaced by ugly corrugated iron. So far, at least, this has not happened on a wide scale in Santana, and government incentive schemes exist to encourage the older people of Santana to maintain their traditional houses and lifestyle.

Colourful, and surprisingly spacious; Madeiran houses and one cowshed (above)

Building castles with discarded maize husks; playtime in Arco de São Jorge

SÃO JORGE

Fruit orchards and willow plantations dominate the scenic valleys between São Jorge and its neighbours, Arco de São Jorge and Boaventura. Tourist buses stop at the big As Cabanas shopping and restaurant complex just outside São Jorge, but if you are not interested in embroidery and passion-fruit liqueurs you can visit the pretty baroque church in the village or take a refreshing stroll along the headland to the Ponta de São Jorge lighthouse. From here there are extensive views of the wild northern coastline.

Equally good are the views along the coast road to **Boaventura**. Here the main attraction is the peaceful cemetery set high up above the village church; romantic souls come here to visit the grave of Miss Turner, an American lady who died around 1925. Miss Turner was the owner of a thriving tearoom catering to English visitors in Santo da Serra, noted for its splendid garden. Her gardener would often talk about his home village of Boaventura, describing it as a paradise by the sea, beyond the Madeiran peaks. His descriptions fed her dreams and though she never visited the village, she requested that her mortal remains be buried in the Boaventura cemetery, a wish that was respected, even though it meant carrying her coffin over steep mountain tracks, since roads only came to the area in recent years. *Location: 50km north of Funchal.*

SÃO VICENTE

Most visitors to Madeira have to pass through São Vicente at some time because it is located at the junction of the island's spectacular north coast road and the main road to Ribeira Brava in the south. In an attempt to persuade travellers to stop and even stay a night or two, considerable sums have been spent on building new hotels and restaurants and smartening the town up, so that it sparkles with an almost-too-pristine cleanliness, its buildings whitewashed to dazzling brightness.

The old town still has considerable charm, with its small, typically Madeiran general stores selling everything from pungent salt cod to religious statues. The simple parish church has colourful tiles and a painted ceiling. The modern church of Nossa Senhora de Fátima stands high on a hill above the town, built between 1942 and 1953 with an eye-catching belltower. There is also a tiny chapel built in 1692, by the bridge at the mouth of the São Vicente river, which you will see if you head west to Porto Moniz on the north coast road.

The only village along this wild and lonely road is tiny **Seixal** where the hardy villagers manage to produce excellent wine, despite the Atlantic gales. The miniscule vineyards set in the steep hillside are protected from the worst of the winds by little shelter belts of dried bracken and heather. Near Seixal you will see the splendid waterfall known to locals as 'the windy skirt', because of the way that it billows out from the high clifftop before tumbling down in a thin cascade to the rocks below.

Just before Porto Moniz, you will catch sight of the *janela* (window) in the offshore rocks, a feature which gives its name to the lush and scenic Ribeira da Janela ravine which cuts up to Rabaçal and Paúl da Serra. If you have four hours to spare, there is a rewarding walk up this valley, following the Levada da Central da Ribeira da Janela from the car park and reservoir just above the village of Lamaceiros.

Location: 55km north of Funchal.

São Vicente's ancient chapel and old town district tempt travellers to stop

FLOWERS

Bougainvillea (left) turning Funchal's rivers red; Golden Trumpet (*Atlamanda cathartica*) from South America (above); Indian fig tree and Mediterranean hibiscus (right); South African Bird of Paradise (*Strelitzia*) and tropical orchid (far right)

Madeira's roadside verges, *levada* paths and public parks are bright with flowers throughout the year. Thanks to the introduction of so many South African plants, which bloom in the depths of the northern hemisphere's winter, the botanical interest can be just as great in December as in August, and visitors arriving for Christmas festivities are greeted by rampant red agave flowers lining the airport road into Funchal.

Some flowers bloom all year in Madeira's equable climate, including oleanders, red and orange-flowered hibiscus and the aptly named Bird of Paradise (*Strelitzia reginae*) with its pointed, crest-like inflorescences – other winter-flowering plants include poinsettias, introduced from South America, with their scarlet leaves and gold stamens, camellias, orchids and arum lilies.

The many different varieties of

mimosa that grow in the island's woods are also covered in powder-puff yellow flowers at this time of year. This woodland display is bettered only by the flowering of the jacaranda trees in central Funchal in April and May. Planted along all Funchal's main roads, their massed blossoms form a river of lilac blue when viewed from above – descending from the hotel district, for example. Even as the jacaranda blossoms drop, the Pride of Bolivia (*Tipuana tipu*) picks up the baton, flowering in Avenida Zarco from June through much of the summer.

Summer is the season of massed agapanthus, growing wild along the waysides, of fragrant giant honeysuckles, of the even sweeter frangipani and literally hundreds of other plants. Some will seem familiar, most of them wonderfully exotic – if you want a basic illustrated guide, *The Plants and Flowers of Madeira*, by António da Costa and Luis de O Franquinho, is good value for money and widely available on the island.

Western Madeira Drive

This all-day tour of western Madeira will take you along the sunny southern coast, up to the contrasting moorlands of the Paúl da Serra and down to Porto Moniz, returning along the spectacular north coast road and the Encumeada mountain pass.

THE SOUTH COAST ROAD

Leave Funchal on the EN101 passing through the Estrada Monumental Hotel Zone and reaching the picturesque fishing village of **Câmara de Lobos** (see page 80–1), through a sea of banana plantations, giving way to grapevines on the higher slopes. After another 7km you will reach **Cabo Girão** (page 76–7); those with a good head for heights can stop here to look

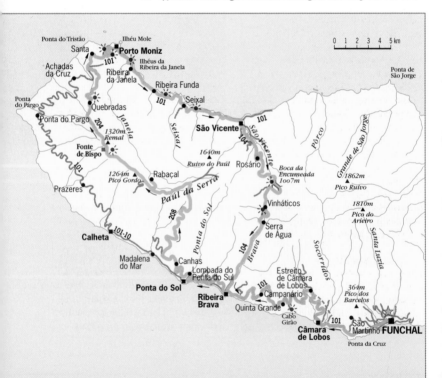

down to the sea from the top of one of the world's highest cliffs (550m) marvelling at the bravery and tenacity of the farmers who have cut little terraces into the face. The next stop, after 11km, is **Ribeira Brava** (page 106) where you can stop for coffee, wander through the harbourside market and visit São Bento, one of the island's oldest and most interesting churches.

From here, ignore the right turn to São Vicente and carry on along the EN101 coastal road. After 3km the road divides – stay on the lower road which runs alongside the beach and through tunnels below steep cliffs to which tiny terraces cling. **Ponta do Sol** (page 100–1) is so called because it gets the sun all day, not being overshadowed by high mountains; hence you will see bananas grown everywhere, and packing stations where this economically important crop is processed for export. Turn right here (ignoring the EN101-10). After 3km you will reach **Canhas**, an important pilgrimage centre with a Via Sacra (Holy Way, or Stations of the Cross) running up through the village to a huge crucifix. Come here on the first Sunday in the month and you will encounter crowds of festive islanders at open-air mass. Next to the crucifix is an abandoned housing estate – islanders will give you different explanations for this ghost town (built by someone who won the national lottery, say some; built by Venezuelan oil millionaires say others – in any event, the money ran out).

PAÚL DA SERRA

Just west of Canhas you will meet the only dead straight stretch of road on Madeira. After 3km, turn right and drive 12km to the road junction at the top of the Paúl da Serra plateau (page 94). Bear left on the EN204 towards Porto Moniz. After 5km you can divert right to Rabaçal for the Risco Waterfall Walk (page 120). The road across the bleak Paúl da Serra is raised above the moorland because of frequent flooding. You will not see many other people, but you will see grazing sheep, goats and cows, and wind turbines built to generate electricity.

PORTO MONIZ

Porto Moniz (page 102) is reached after 25km. As you descend into this small north coast village, do not miss the viewpoint on the right from which you can look down on a pattern of tiny fields hedged with bracken. There are several good fish restaurants in the village. Porto Moniz is the start point for a spectacular drive along the north coast, through Seixal to São Vicente. The 19km road took 16 years to build and consists of tunnels cut through the cliffs and ledges hacked out of the cliffside offering intimate views of Atlantic breakers below and cascading waterfalls above.

BOCA DA ENCUMEADA

At São Vicente (page 114–5) take the EN104 right which climbs 12km up to the Encumeada Pass (page 76). Here a viewpoint allows you to look north and south down the two great ravines which almost split the island into two parts. After another 4km you will pass one of the island's two *pousadas*, or government-owned inns, the Pousada dos Vinháticos (named after Madeira's native tree). Just below is another viewpoint from which you can look down on to a green and unspoiled valley, its sides sculpted into hundreds of tiny terraces. After 10km you will return to Ribeira Brava; turn left and retrace the morning's journey back to Funchal.

Risco Waterfall Walk

Risco waterfall is one of the most scenic spots on Madeira, and the short walk to the fall is well worth doing as a break from your tour of the west of the island. *Allow 30 minutes.*

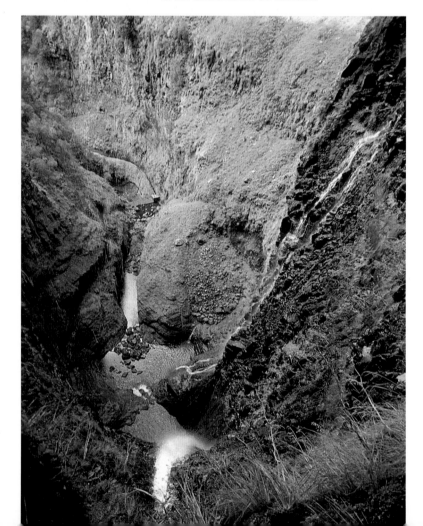

RABAÇAL

To reach the start point of the walk, take the EN204, following the signs for Porto Moniz as you cross the empty moorland that characterises the Paúl da Serra plateau. Look for the sharp turning right that leads steeply downhill to Rabaçal. Take great care along this road because it is only wide enough for one vehicle – use your horn at blind corners to warn other motorists of your presence. If you meet another vehicle, it is usual for the one climbing uphill to reverse back to the nearest passing place. A short way down the road, you will drive across a river bed, albeit a very shallow one. This is the Ribeira do Alecrim (meaning Rosemary River) named after the rosemary that grows along its pretty banks and pools. After 2km you will come to a small car-park, next to a government resthouse, which has picnic tables and a terrace. This is Rabaçal, a delightful spot whose name means something like virgin, primeval or unspoiled, and looking out from the terrace over the green valley below it is not difficult to see why it has been given this name.

LEVADA DO RISCO

From the car-park, follow the dirt track that leads downhill (on the right as you face the resthouse). Very soon this will bring you down to the Levada do Risco, which follows the valley side at a height of 1,030m.

The woodland either side of the *levada* is magical: the gnarled trees are hung with great hanks of lime green lichen, and wild goats feed among the many tumbled

The view from the Levada do Risco. High rainfall and humidity encourages the lush valley greenery and the growth of different types of lichen and moss

boulders that lie scattered across the hillside. The undergrowth consists of tree heath (*Erica arborea*); lying around the path you can pick up branches and roots of this iron-hard plant, brought down by storms or landslips – the wood is used all over Madeira for fencing and it used to be carved to make yokes for carrying goatskins full of grape juice or wine in the days before motorised transport.

LEVADA DOS 25 FONTES

Following the path you will pass a signposted junction – the way left leads downhill and then right to the spot known as Vinte e Cinco Fontes (25 Springs). You can return later, if you wish, and take this path which leads, after about one hour, to a pool into which tumble numerous little waterfalls. The route to Risco continues straight ahead, and as you pass along the path, sweeping views open up on the left, looking down the green and unspoiled valley of the Ribeira Grande.

RISCO WATERFALL

The sound of the waterfall will greet you before you see it. Just before the fall, the path divides – keep to the right, climbing up the concrete wall of the *levada* and ignoring the wider path to the left (this path leads a short way downhill to a reservoir then stops). Rounding a corner, you will see the fall, its waters cascading from a height of 100m. If it is a hot day and you have brought a bathing costume you can walk behind the fall (getting soaked in the process) to view it from the other side, though you cannot walk any further, since the *levada* ends here. Despite getting wet you will soon dry in the warmth as you return along the footpath to Rabaçal.

Central Madeira Drive

If you only have time for one drive on Madeira, this is the one. It will take a whole day but is very varied, taking in burnt volcanic wastes, lush green valleys, wave-battered coasts, and traditional island architecture and crafts.

TO MONTE

From Funchal, head north out of the city, following Rua 31 de Janeiro (ie, the right bank of the Ribeira de Santa Luzia). Follow the signs to Monte (page 90) which you will reach after 5km. Having paid your respects to the former Emperor Charles I of Austro-Hungary, entombed in Monte church, and watched nervous passengers setting off on the Monte toboggan run, continue north on the EN103 for 3km to Terreiro da Luta and visit the statue of the Virgin on her 5.5m column, built as a World War I memorial.

PICO DO ARIEIRO

After 3km look for a byroad to the left which takes you through one of the island's national parks (if you miss the turning just go on to Poiso and turn left). Emerging from the park turn left for 4km to reach Pico do Arieiro (page 95), the island's third highest peak. The landscape in the nature park and on the peak is volcanic. Little grows on the rusty red laterite soil, though a major reafforestation programme is now under way – the forestry department faces an additional problem in the number of rabbits which contrive to denude what little vegetation grows here, including recently planted tree seedlings. At the peak you can break for refreshments and take a walk among the magnificent volcanic formations (see page 96).

RIBEIRO FRIO

Backtrack to Poiso (the Abrigo do Poiso restaurant here is excellent if you fancy lunch), then take the EN103 left to Ribeiro Frio (page 108), where you can watch the trout playing in the crystal clear waters of the local fish farm. Heading on along the EN103, you will pass through Achada do Cedro Gordo, whose name refers to the abundant crab apple trees grown for cider production, then through Cruzinhas, Lombo de Cima, Degolada and Faial. This route passes through gentle agricultural scenery, highly fertile, where the local farmers can grow produce all year round, producing three, or even four, crops a year of beans, potatoes, carrots, cabbages or maize.

SANTANA

The beautiful landscape from Faial to Santana is dotted with thatched cowsheds and traditional Madeiran houses (page 112), the difference between which is scarcely more than a lick of bright paint. You can inspect these A-framed houses more closely in Santana (page 110) where one is open to the public. Returning along the road to Faial, look out for dwarf willow trees, deliberately polled to produce willow whips for wickerwork. You may also see bundles of stripped willow stacked against houses. From Faial, heading along the EN101, the view ahead is dominated by the huge flat-topped Eagle Rock (Penha deÁguia), rising to 590m. Porto da Cruz has a pebbled beach and you can swim in the deep clean waters of the little harbour.

CAMACHA

From Porto da Cruz, the EN101 takes you to Portela, with good views back to Eagle Rock from the terrace next to the village bar. Continuing along the EN102 for 16km you will reach Camacha, the centre of the island's willow weaving industry (pages 80 and 147). The huge store next to the Café Relogio on the main square has a vast range of wicker goods for sale and you can watch weavers at work. From Camacha, the well-signposted EN102 and EN101 roads will take you back to Funchal.

A typical Madeira scene: meticulously tended fields producing year-round crops

Mountain Peaks

You can drive to the summit of Madeira's third highest peak, Pico do Arieiro (1,810m) in under an hour from central Funchal. Having arrived, the magnificent panoramas will tempt all but the most lethargic to take a walk.

The 3-hour walk from here to Madeira's highest peak, Pico Ruivo (1,862m) is rated one of the most spectacular on Madeira, but the going is very steep and only recommended to expert walkers, properly equipped. Non-experts can undertake the first 30 minutes of the walk provided that the weather is good and that you have good non-slip walking shoes. You will also need a sweater and/or a windproof jacket in the winter months.

The walk begins to the left of the pousada, marked by a big yellow sign saying 'Pico Ruivo 10km'.

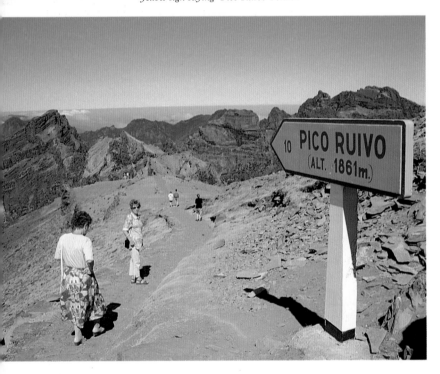

PICO DO ARIEIRO

You can spend the night on the summit of this mountain if you book in advance at the Pousada do Pico do Arieiro (tel: 230110), the government-owned inn; the advantage is the opportunity to watch the sunset, gaze at the night sky away from the glare of city lights, and then observe the most spectacular dawn. Even if you do not make it here early enough for sunrise, you can get a taste of its colours at most times of the day because the sunlight, playing on the orange, purple, pink and brown volcanic rocks, makes their colours all the more intense.

TO VIEWPOINT ONE

The first part of the walk follows a well-paved path and the principal ingredients are silence (except for the wind) and spectacular views of deep cliffs and ravines on every side. The eerie silence continues as you approach the first *miradouro*, or viewpoint, and the sense of isolation is increased by the clouds that often cling to the valleys way beneath your feet, cutting you off from the sights and sounds of the noisy, busy world below. The view from the first *miradouro* is dominated by the long ridge of Pico das Torres (Peak of the Towers) to the north – so called because of the tower-like lumps and columns running up the jagged ridge to Madeira's second highest peak (1,851m).

TO VIEWPOINT TWO

The path now curls round, taking you to the western, and more sheltered, side of a cliff to which a few disc-shaped house leeks cling, growing out of the cinder-like rock. Here you overlook the great gorge

Setting out from Pico do Arieiro for the summit of Pico Ruivo

The mountain panorama seen from the Pico do Arieiro viewpoint

of Ribeiro do Cidrão. In the distance, ahead and to the left is the great plateau of the Paúl da Serra rising above the clouds, marked by giant electricity generating windmills with their huge propeller blades.

If you suffer from vertigo, this is probably as far as you should go. The 10-minute walk to the next viewpoint is very steep and at times the path is no more than a 2m-wide spine of rock, with sheer drops on either side – though there are iron railings and wire ropes to hold on to if you need help.

From the second *miradouro* you can just see Pico Ruivo to the left, while Funchal may just be visible on a clear day, 22km away. Turning round, you can see Pico do Arieiro far above, to which you now must return; don't worry – it is not such hard work as it looks, and you should be back at the café on the peak for a well-earned drink within half an hour.

Eastern Madeira Drive

The eastern part of Madeira is the most developed but it also has historic towns and dramatic seascapes. *This tour can be done in half a day but it is better to take it at a more leisurely pace, perhaps stopping for a picnic or a swim.*

QUINTA DO PALHEIRO

Leave Funchal on the EN101 east, signposted to the airport, but turn left after 3km on the EN102 signposted to Camacha. After 2km turn right on the byroad signposted 'Quinta do Palheiro'. After 1km you will reach the *quinta* on the right, where you can easily spend an hour walking round the lovingly tended gardens (page 104). Leaving the *quinta*, turn right, then first left, and then right again to rejoin the EN102. This will take you to **Camacha** (page 80) where you can stop and shop for wickerwork if you have not already paid a visit.

SANTO DA SERRA

Continue along the EN102 for another 11km and you will reach Santo António da Serra (page 108) with its miniature zoo and extensive park, known locally as the camellia garden,

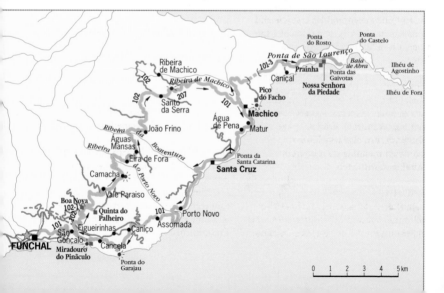

though plenty of other plants grow here as well. The road from Santo da Serra is dotted with holiday villas. Turn left after 1.6km, then right after 2.2km, rejoining the EN101 westwards, signposted to Machico. After 6km, before reaching Machico, turn left on the EN101-3 signposted to Caniçal and the Zona Franca Industrial. The road passes through a newly made tunnel, whose purpose is revealed as you skirt Caniçal heading for Ponta de São Lourenço – just east of Caniçal is a new industrial estate, a blot on the landscape, but designed to keep industry out of built-up residential districts. The industrial estate occupies the site of the island's now-redundant whale processing factory (see page 130).

PONTA DE SÃO LOURENÇO

Soon you will pass the artificial landscape of the industrial zone and return to volcanic rocks in various shades of orange and brown. A sign to the right after 1.5km points to Prainha, the location of the island's only naturally sandy beach, a place for swimming in the turquoise-coloured seas. At the end of the road, you can walk out along the rugged headland of Ponta de São Lourenço (see page 128) for wonderful views. In the car park two old men sell trinkets made from discarded whalebone. To learn more about this now defunct industry, you can visit the whaling museum in Caniçal (page 84), where you can also watch tuna fishermen mending their boats or bringing in the catch.

MACHICO

A short drive back along the EN101-3 will bring you to Machico (page 88), the ancient capital of the eastern part of the

island, now a buzzing resort town. Worth visiting is the Manueline-style parish church and the peaceful cemetery just down hill from the Dom Pedro Baía hotel, a spot colonised by some of the island's most spectacular flowers.

SANTA CRUZ

The road from Machico to Santa Cruz passes under the airport runway, which is built up on huge concrete pillars, and if a plane is coming in it may seem about to land on your car roof! In Santa Cruz (page 108) the tower of the 16th-century

The sun sets over Ponta de São Lourenço

parish church beckons; it is joined on the same square by the equally ancient Câmara Municipal, or town hall.

CANIÇO

The last stop before you return to Funchal, Caniço (page 85) has the appearance of a developed resort village, but you should continue down to the coast at Ponta do Garajau, not so much for the outsize statue of Christ as for the beach area with its views, its coloured rocks and the stands of prickly pear cactus. From the beach, turn left at the first junction to rejoin the EN101 Funchal road at Cancela.

Ponta de São Lourenço Walk

This walk provides a breathing space on your tour of eastern Madeira – a place to stop off and spend an hour exploring the massive cliffs and lonely bays at the very tip of the island, while aeroplanes fly overhead going in and out of Santa Catarina airport.

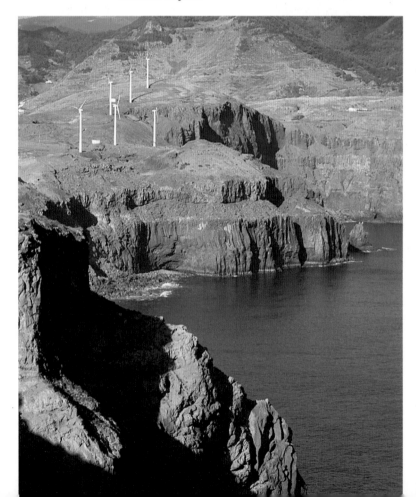

Developments around Caniçal to create the industrial free port have tamed the landscape as you approach the island's easternmost point, but you will then pass through a lunar landscape of burnt orange and chocolate brown soils as you approach the end of the tarmac road. Here you can leave the car and climb up the rocks to the right of the car park to a picnic area with tables and chairs and a panoramic view of the Baia de Abra, and the Ilhas Desertas (Deserted Isles) in the distance.

THE WALK

Two rusty iron posts by the car park mark the beginning of the walk. Shortly afterwards the track divides – ignore the wide track that leads upwards and straight ahead; instead bear right, and downhill, to the bottom of a shallow valley, then up the other side, keeping the wide view of the bay to your right.

As you climb the ridge ahead the views become more and more dramatic, and the sunshine heightens the vivid colours of the striped cliff-faces on your right, resembling a section through a giant layer cake.

FLORA

The dry thin soil of this headland supports a different mix of plants to other parts of the island, including some noble members of the often-maligned thistle family. You may see *Silybum marianum*, the milk thistle, which has bold white-veined leaves and striking flowers. Another very prickly specimen is the horned, or Mexican, poppy (*Argemone mexicana*), with its big papery yellow flowers and bright orange sap. The most abundant of the thistles

Modern wind turbines contrast with the primeval ruggedness of the volcanic landscape at the island's eastern tip

here is the prickly cardoon (*Eynara cardunculus*), a relative of the artichoke with big sweetly scented flowers much visited by bees and other insects.

VIEWS

After 20 minutes gentle uphill climbing you will reach a drystone wall built of boulders, with a gap for walkers to pass through. Beyond this point there are scores of tracks eroded by sheep and visitors – bear leftwards, descending gradually across the bare biscuit-coloured bedrock. Before long you will reach a flat area with views to the left down a rock ravine. Down below, Atlantic waves dash against the raw red cliffs of the island's north face.

If you like you can take a path to the left that gives access to an even more breathtaking view, but only for those with a head for heights. From here on the path is more easy to follow. It leads eastwards to a ridge on which a telegraph pole sits – you are not aiming for the pole itself, but the rock platform higher up to the left of it.

Here you can sit and admire views that stretch far in every direction. To the east you can see the lighthouse on the tip of Ilhéu de Fora, the island at the easternmost tip of Madeira. Further to the right is an eyelet or window in the rocky headland called Ponta do Furado, and beyond that, the flat-topped Ilhas Desertas (Deserted Isles) are normally visible (if not, local lore says it will soon rain).

This is a very different Madeira from the green, flower-filled interior of the island, bleak and inhospitable but none the less beautiful. Here you can enjoy real solitude, alone with the buzzards, hawks and other birds of prey that you may see wheeling overhead as you return to the car park at the start of the walk.

WHALING & CONSERVATION

Visitors to Ponta de São Lourenço will see old men selling trinkets made of whalebone ivory, the last sad remnants of an industry that is no more, for the hunting and killing of whales finally stopped in Madeiran waters in June 1981. Now there is a proposal to turn the waters of the archipelago into a marine reserve for ocean mammals – not just sperm whales, but also the dolphins that are still hunted for their meat and the monk seals that are persecuted because they are perceived as competing with Madeira's fishermen for commercial fish stocks. If the scheme is realised, the sight of sperm whales playing in the waters off Madeira may once again become relatively common. That, at least, is the hope of marine biologists working for the Society for the Protection of Sea Mammals who have been conducting research into whale migration in Madeiran waters since 1985. It is heartening to report that the researchers are being greatly aided by former whaling fishermen who are now using their knowledge and experience of the sperm whales' habits to help protect the very same creatures that they used to hunt.

Relics of an extinct industry: scrimshaws and boats carved from whale ivory

GETTING AWAY FROM IT ALL

*God created the world
and was so pleased
with His work that He
gave it a kiss and Madeira
was born.*
MADEIRAN MYTH

Taking a boat trip gives you a different perspective on Madeira's dramatic scenery

BOAT TRIPS

Madeira is rich territory for those who want to get away from it all, an island of wild places and endless meandering footpaths (see page 136). Another way to escape is to head for the sea; by joining a mini cruise you can see the island's towering cliffs from a different perspective and returning to Funchal harbour you will retrace the sea route taken by all visitors to Madeira in the past, before the first commercial aeroplane services began in 1964.

The wind and the sea

The best half-day excursions by boat take you along the island's southern coast, either to Baia de Abra, to the east, or westwards to Ponta do Sol, passing the foot of Cabo Girão, one of the world's highest sea cliffs. Some operators anchor off the island for a while so that you can

swim – the waters are very clean and the sea temperature is rarely less than 18°C even in December and January. Evening excursions are available as well, timed to make the most of the sunset. Most operators use motor boats but you can also spend a day at sea under sail on the 20m yacht *Albatroz*, built in 1939 and beautifully restored. All boat excursions depart from Funchal's yacht marina and you can either book direct at the marina offices, or through hotels and travel agents.

THE ILHAS DESERTAS

For the ultimate away-from-it-all experience you can join one of the occasional boat trips that go to the Ilhas Desertas, the three flat islands that stand 20km to the southeast of Madeira. The largest of the islands, Deserta Grande, is a long narrow plateau of volcanic rock measuring 12km by 1km and rising to 479m in height. The island is arid and the soil too thin to support crops, though it is home to the very rare big wolf spider (*Lycosa ingens*), which is black, ferocious and so poisonous that its bite can cause death to humans. All attempts to inhabit Deserta Grande have been shortlived, though there is a biological observatory on the island, manned by naturalists. Their job is to monitor and protect the wildlife, notably a small colony of monk seals. The seals were once more numerous but raids by Madeiran fisherman resulted in mass slaughter and their near extinction – the fishermen regarded the fish-eating seals as a threat to their livelihood. The fishermen also killed half the island's bird population in another raid in 1976. To prevent further bloodshed, the island was declared a nature reserve in 1990. Visitors can now land only with a special permit, granted exclusively to people engaged in legitimate research projects. You can, however, sail to the islands to watch the seals, and you may also catch sight of dolphins and turtles. There are also many sea birds to be seen around the islands, including Cory's, Manx and the Madeiran little shearwater, plus Bulwer's, soft-plumaged and Madeiran petrels (a visit to Funchal's Municipal Museum, page 52, will help you identify all of these).

Turipesca (tel: 231063) and Costa do Sol (tel: 238538), both based in Funchal's marina, offer charter boat tours to the Ilhas Desertas and you should also enquire at the tourist office about trips aboard the government-owned yacht Pirata Azul.

SPORT FISHING

Big fish abound in the deep waters off Madeira and regular excursions depart

Madeira waters teem with fish

from Funchal's marina in search of marlin, tuna, swordfish and shark. If you happen to be passing the marina when the fishing boats come in, you can watch the proud anglers posing for a photograph with their catch alongside a chalk board that records the length and weight of the prize.

Trips can be arranged through travel agents or through Turipesca (tel: 231063) and Costa do Sol (tel: 238538).

UNDERSEA EXPLORATION

For those who prefer to watch and admire the strange creatures of the deep, rather than hunt them, there are several diving centres on Madeira and on Porto Santo. Scorpio Divers (*Complexo do Lido, Funchal, tel: 266977*) takes on everyone, from absolute beginners to experienced divers, and is a British-run sub-aqua club with fully trained and certified instructors, based in Funchal's Hotel Zone.

Atalaia, based in Caniço, offers equipment hire and courses (tel: 933334) as does the Urs Moser Diving School (tel: 982162) on the island of Porto Santo (see page 140), but only from May to October.

SEA LIFE

If you have never been diving before in your life, Madeira is the place to have a go, with several schools catering for absolute beginners (see page 133). The clear blue seas round Madeira's southern coast are rich in underwater caves where you can marvel at the variety of the vegetation and the agility of the multi-coloured fish.

Some 4km out from the shore you may encounter hammerhead sharks, big-eye tuna and barracuda, the kind of big fish

the underwater world are the sea anemones that cling to the black basalt rocks of the sea bed, the coral-coloured scorpion fish

that excite sporting anglers and the island's commercial fishermen, but inshore you are not likely to encounter anything more ferocious than a moray eel. Sea bream, mullet, sea perch and garoupa are quite common, as are squid and octopus, but the real gems of

Tuna (above) and jewel-like sea anemones

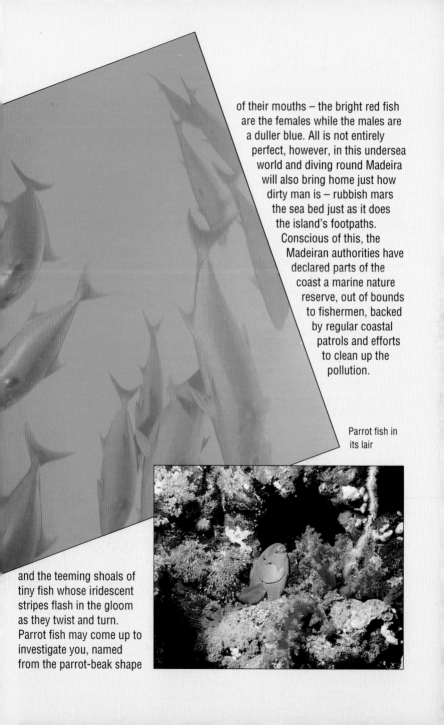

of their mouths – the bright red fish
are the females while the males are
a duller blue. All is not entirely
perfect, however, in this undersea
world and diving round Madeira
will also bring home just how
dirty man is – rubbish mars
the sea bed just as it does
the island's footpaths.
Conscious of this, the
Madeiran authorities have
declared parts of the
coast a marine nature
reserve, out of bounds
to fishermen, backed
by regular coastal
patrols and efforts
to clean up the
pollution.

Parrot fish in
its lair

and the teeming shoals of
tiny fish whose iridescent
stripes flash in the gloom
as they twist and turn.
Parrot fish may come up to
investigate you, named
from the parrot-beak shape

HIKING

There were very few roads on Madeira until the 1960s – instead a complex network of footpaths crisscrossed the island linking up with the equally extensive system of pathways running alongside the island's *levadas*, or irrigation canals (see page 138). These footpaths make Madeira a wonderful place for long-distance walking with all the attractions of panoramic views, waterfalls, scented woodlands, abundant flora and arresting geological formations.

Beginners

Madeira's balmy climate, coupled with the fact that *levada* paths are nice and level, requiring no strenuous up or downhill climbing, are both good reasons why almost anyone can enjoy walking on the island. Four straightforward walks along well-trodden footpaths are detailed in this guide (see pages 72, 120, 124 and 128) and you can also discover the pleasures of *levada* walking by joining guided walks. The specialists in this area are the Sociedade de Animação Turistica (Sitio da Igreja, Camacha, tel: 922288), led by knowledgeable local guides. Their walks can be booked direct or through travel agencies and the tourist office in Funchal.

Footwear and clothing

Despite the apparent ease of walking on Madeira, it is still vital to take proper precautions. In particular, wear proper footwear – mountain boots are not necessary for many *levada* trails but you must wear waterproof shoes that will protect your feet and that do not slip on wet rocks, mossy paths and scree slopes. Madeiran paths can be narrow and slippery, often with steep drops if you fall. Walking in flimsy shoes is asking for trouble, and every year many unprepared visitors suffer injuries serious enough to require hospital

Many beautiful parts of the island are accessible only on foot treatment because they trip or slip over.

Some kind of rain protection – a light windproof cape or cagoule – is also advised, because rain can occur at almost any time of the year, especially around the 700–1,000m level where the clouds tend to hang and on the north side of the island, which bears the brunt of the Atlantic weather fronts. Equally, sun protection is important if you are walking above the cloud level, otherwise you can suffer serious sunburn, especially if you expose your shoulders and neck.

Experienced walkers

The bible for serious walkers on Madeira is John and Pat Underwood's *Landscapes of Madeira*, which is sold in just about every newsagents and souvenir shop on the island. Opinions differ, naturally enough, on which walks are the very best, but if you are short of time, most people agree that the following three are difficult to beat for variety and scenic value:

● Pico do Arieiro to Pico Ruivo (the first part of this route is covered on page 124)
● Rabaçal to the waterfall at Risco and Vinte e Cinco Fontes (part covered on page 120)
● Queimadas to the Caldeirão do Inferno (the Cauldron of Hell! – see page 111).

Planning and precautions

Nothing in the world is ever perfect, and the big drawback for walkers on Madeira is the cost and time involved in getting to and from the start and end points of your walk. Some people get round this by camping or sleeping out under the stars, but adapting this approach you miss one of Madeira's big attractions: the chance to walk all day among mountain peaks

Well worth the effort: the view from Balcões (see page 108)

and then retire at night not to some sweaty alpine hut, but to a comfortable hotel with shower and a good restaurant.

Buses offer a cheap and reliable way of getting to and from your walk but for optimum freedom it is best to hire a car or use a taxi. If you team up with other walkers you can share the cost between four or five – it is, in any case, advisable not to go walking on your own in case you have an accident; if you do go out alone, be sure to tell someone where you are going and what time you can be expected back so that the alarm can be raised if you fail to return.

LEVADAS

Levadas penetrate where no roads go

The *levadas* of Madeira are a unique and endearing feature of the island, forming an astonishing network of irrigation canals, some 2,150km in total length. The earliest canals date right back to the colonisation of the island in the 15th and 16th centuries, though most were dug, entirely by hand, in the early part of the 20th century. Their purpose is to distribute water from those parts of the island that have plenty – notably the north side where average annual rainfall tops 2m – to the dry areas, such as the sunny south where the economically important grape and banana crops are grown. The *levadas* are fed both by natural springs and by reservoirs – giant storage tanks built up in the mountains. Water from the outfalls is first put to work driving the turbines of the island's electricity generating power stations.

Maintaining the *levadas* is an important job, entrusted to the *levadeiro*,

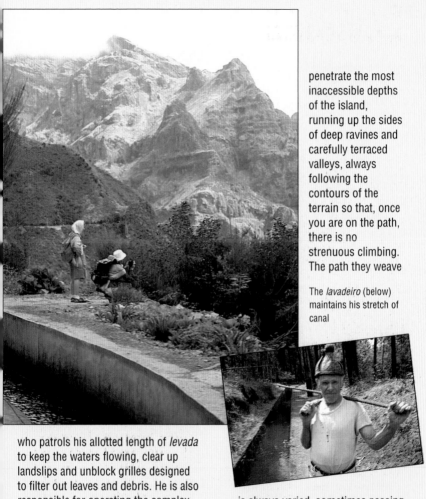

penetrate the most inaccessible depths of the island, running up the sides of deep ravines and carefully terraced valleys, always following the contours of the terrain so that, once you are on the path, there is no strenuous climbing. The path they weave

The *lavadeiro* (below) maintains his stretch of canal

who patrols his allotted length of *levada* to keep the waters flowing, clear up landslips and unblock grilles designed to filter out leaves and debris. He is also responsible for operating the complex system of sluices and watergates which divert water to the individual properties bordering the *levada* according to a carefully worked out schedule. To do this, the *levadeiro* needs access to the water channels – hence the footpaths that run alongside, built for purely functional reasons but coincidentally offering a paradise for walkers. They

is always varied, sometimes passing through rock-cut tunnels, at other times through ancient woodland hung with moss and lichens and sometimes alongside sunny cherry orchards or market gardens. Best of all, they take you to places where the modern world has yet to penetrate, far from the sound of traffic, but full of the sounds of birds and gently running water.

PORTO SANTO

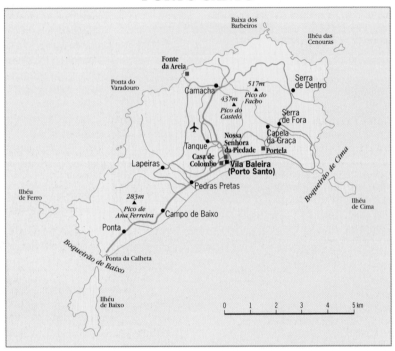

PORTO SANTO

If sun, sea and sand are what you are looking for, then you probably will not have chosen Madeira for your holiday. Porto Santo, on the other hand, has all three and not much else. Porto Santo's 9km-long sandy beach runs almost the entire length of the island's southern coast. Anywhere else in Europe this beach would now be backed by scores of high-rise hotels – as it is, sheer remoteness has ensured that Porto Santo's beach remains undeveloped and unspoilt, a paradise for those who enjoy idle sunbathing or more active water sports, such as wind surfing.

Getting there

There are several flights a day between Santa Catarina airport and Porto Santo. The 37km journey takes a mere 15 minutes. The price is quite high but flights are often fully booked in the summer season, so it is advisable to book in advance through TAP (Air Portugal), Avenida das Comunidades Madeirenses 10 (tel: 239200) or through a travel agent.

The journey by sea, in a turbo-driven catamaran, takes between an hour and a half and two hours, depending on the weather. When conditions are anything but calm, people susceptible to seasickness will not enjoy the journey and should fly. Again bookings can be made through any travel agent, or direct with the operators, whose office fronts on to the yacht marina (tel: 227020). There are two sailings each way every day in summer and one in winter, timed so that day trippers get around 6 hours on the island.

Getting around

It is a 20-minute walk or a very short taxi ride from the ferry port or airport to the beach and to Vila Baleira, Porto Santo's only town. If you want to tour the island, taxis can be hired at the ports or in Vila Baleira. Alternatively you can rent a car, book a boat trip round the island or join a guided tour; just head for the seafront shops in Vila Baleira and you will find all these options on offer. For the more adventurous, the Urs Moser Diving Centre hires out bicycles and motorcycles as well as organising diving and boat trips; they are at Rua João Gonçalves 5, Vila Baleira (tel: 982162).

Porto Santo's seemingly endless ribbon of sand, one of Europe's last unspoiled beaches

The island's character

Porto Santo is a pretty uncomplicated place for most of the year – it only gets crowded in August when Madeirans flock over for their annual holiday. The airport, which serves as a reserve NATO airbase, saw action during the Falklands campaign and the Gulf War but for most of the time the island's inhabitants enjoy a peaceful existence, tending tiny plots where figs, melons, grapes and pumpkins are grown. Windmills dot the hilltops; mostly modern ones these days for generating electricity, although there is at least one ancient structure with canvas sails, still grinding corn in the traditional manner. Donkeys are used for transport and the upland areas are grazed by cattle and sheep. Overall, the island looks brown and arid but there are springs on the island feeding the irrigation system, and one of them produces bottled mineral waters.

History

Apart from the fact that Porto Santo was the first island to be 'discovered' by Zarco in 1418 (see page 10) it is more famous for two other things: Columbus and prophets.

Columbus married the daughter of the island's first governor (see page 13) and may have lived on Porto Santo for a period: the story is told at the Casa de Colombo (House of Columbus) at Rua Cristovão Colombo 12 (open Monday to Friday, 10am–noon and 2pm–5.30pm).

As for prophets (*profetas*) that is the name which the local pop group has

adopted in memory of a 16th-century islander and his niece who claimed miraculous powers: disconcertingly, they were able to itemise a person's past sins in some detail, and they set up their own fanatical religious movement on the island until the Church got to hear of it and had them arrested. Although this all happened as far back as 1533, Madeirans still refer contemptuously to their neighbours as '*profetas*'.

Touring Porto Santo

Tours of Porto Santo normally take in one or both of the island's volcanic cones; one is the Pico do Castelo (Castle Peak), so called because it was once fortified as a defence against pirates; the other is Pico do Facho (Torch Peak), the island's highest point (517m), where sentries once lit warning beacons if pirates were sighted. There are wonderful views from both hilltops, sometimes as far as Madeira. Fonte da Areia (Sand Spring) is where the island's mineral water is bottled, the natural spring rising out of the sandstone which has been much eroded by the wind and waves. Serra de Dentro is an uninhabited village, picturesque in its decay, where sheep now graze the vegetation that cloaks the abandoned terraces.

Staying on

If you are hooked on Porto Santo's lazy lifestyle, or want to put in some serious sun worship, the place to stay is the luxurious Porto Santo Hotel (tel: 982381) in Vila Baleira, where the facilities include windsurfing equipment for hire, tennis courts, a swimming pool and a good restaurant.

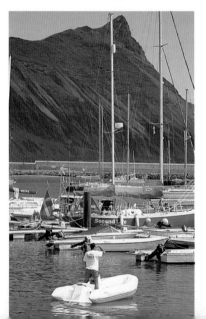

Volcanic peaks tower over Porto Santo's yachting marina

DIRECTORY

The beauty of Madeira will
remain in your heart forever.
MADEIRAN FOLK SONG

Shopping

*P*art of the pleasure of shopping on Madeira is watching your souvenirs being made before you buy. Factories producing embroidery or wickerwork put on demonstrations, and they don't make you feel obliged to buy anything. In fact Madeiran shopkeepers do not go in for high-pressure sales techniques at all and the welcome absence of hassle only adds to the pleasure of browsing through Funchal's many shops.

The best shops are located in the streets immediately north and south of the cathedral. If you are exploring this area, don't forget to look down the little side alleys, as well as the main streets, where some of the most characterful shops are tucked away.

PRACTICAL DETAILS
Shops are open from 9am to 1pm and 3pm to 7pm Monday to Friday,

mornings only on Saturday. Most of them operate under the Tax Free Shopping scheme whereby visitors from outside the European Union can reclaim the IVA (Value Added Tax), which can be anything from 12 to 16 per cent of the purchase price. The scheme only applies for goods costing 11,200 *escudos* or more, but you can easily spend that much on a piece of embroidery. Most retailers can arrange for bulky items to be shipped home for you, but you can just as easily take them home on the plane – airlines are used to passengers flying out of Madeira loaded up with wickerwork or flower boxes. They should be checked in with your main luggage but they will be placed in the aircraft's 'fragile' hold and delivered to you by hand at the airport on your arrival home.

WHAT TO BUY AND WHERE
Antiques
Furniture, mirrors, copper pans, old *azulejos* tiles or even handcarved crib figures – all these are worth looking out for in the little cluster of antique shops that you will find opposite São Pedro church.

Books
If you run out of books to read by the

Portuguese leatherwork is renowned for quality and is keenly priced hotel pool, you can buy all the latest English bestsellers at the **Patio Bookshop**, Rua da Carreira 43 (at the entrance to the Museu Photographia Vicentes). The shop also sells guidebooks and usually has a small stock of illustrated antiquarian guides to Madeira; these make an unusual souvenir and bring back a sense of the island's recent British 'colonial' past.

Bolo do mel

If you get hooked on Madeira's solid and filling honey cake you can buy supplies to take home at numerous *pastelaria*, or baker's shops, such as the one at Rua da Carreira 75. The cake will keep for many months but traditionally a new batch is made on 8 December ready for the Christmas festivities, and any old cake is eaten up on the same day.

Boots

Traditional Madeiran leather boots, with a turned-down top, can be bought from roadside stalls and souvenir shops all over Madeira. If you want to watch them being made, visit **Gonçalves & Silva's** workshop at Rua do Portão de São Tiago 22, in the Zona Velha (Old Town).

Embroidery

Handmade embroidery (*bordados*) is one of the island's most important exports (see page 38) and there is a huge choice of shops all over Funchal stocking the genuine product, as well as cheap machine-made imitations. Genuine handmade embroidery always carries a lead tag fixed to one corner as a guarantee of quality awarded by the island's handicraft institute, **IBTAM** (see page 36). In any case you will soon learn to recognise the genuine article, which is very elegant but also rather

Exquisitely embroidered, but beware of imported machine-made copies

expensive, being a labour intensive product. Some of the big exporters welcome visitors to their factory showrooms where you can watch the pattern printing processes and the final finishing of garments and table linen. One of the best is **Patricio & Gouveia**, at Rua do Visconde de Anadia 33. The biggest choice is to be found, appropriately enough, in Rua dos Murcas (Mercers' Street), where every other shop sells embroidery.

Flowers

Shopping for flowers in the Mercado dos Lavradores, or Workers' Market (see page 44), can be great fun, but it is best to buy from a florist if you want your flowers packed in special boxes for travelling. **A Rosa**, Rua Imperatriz D Amélia 126 (behind the Savoy Hotel in the Hotel Zone), will pack and deliver freshly cut flowers to your hotel if you order them two or three days before departure. Popular, long-lasting Madeiran flowers include orchids (in season from late November to May), strelitzias (birds of paradise) and anthuriums (flamingo flowers), the last two available all year. You can also take home bulbs, seeds and baby orchid plants (see page 42) provided that there is no soil with them.

Cottons come in all colours and designs

Long-lasting Madeiran cut flowers

Food

Gourmets will enjoy browsing in little delicatessens such as the one at Rua do Carmo 11. Best buys are Portuguese olive oil, fresh walnuts in season and *lapas escabeche*, limpets preserved in brine and vinegar, an unusual ingredient for a seafood salad or pasta sauce.

Hats

Bobble hats with earflaps, as worn by Madeiran farmers to keep off the rain, or straw boaters, as worn by Monte toboggan drivers, can always be bought from roadside stalls or try **Salão Londrino**, Rua dos Ferreiros 128.

Leather

Shoes, bags, belts and clothing, mostly imported from the Portuguese mainland, are very good value compared with prices in the fashion shops of northern Europe. To see a good range of stock visit **Pele**, Rua dos Murcas 26, or **Arte Couro**, Rua da Alfândega 15. For really up-market but still affordable products, the best stockists are; **Charles**, Largo do Chafariz 22; **Yaya**, Rua Câmara Pestana 3; **Godiva**, Avenida Arriaga 11–13; **Chloé**, Largo do Phelps 12.

Knitwear

Knitted cotton sweaters and cardigans

are another bargain – you will see them sold at wayside stalls to visitors who discover how much colder it can be in Madeira's mountains. In Funchal you can see a good selection at Rua dos Murcas 4.

Pottery, porcelain, glass and home furnishings

Casa Turistica, in Rua do Conselheiro José Silvestre Ribeiro, is a must for all kinds of souvenirs, but especially for ceramics – whether you just want a cachepot for your potted plants or a full dinner service. The shop is laid out like a cross between a private mansion and a museum, with antiques and oil paintings beneath ornate plastered ceilings as the background for excellent displays. Other good stores selling contemporary Portuguese designs, in textile, pottery, furniture or glass, include **Cayres**, Rua Dr Fernão Ornelas 56, and **Galeria das Louças**, in Rua do Sabão.

Souvenirs

Among the less expensive are dolls in Madeiran costume musical instruments, such as the percussive *brinquinho*, videotapes of the island and miniature bottles of island liqueurs. **Madeira Sun**, Avenida Zarco 4, sells all the typical souvenirs, as does the **Bazar Monte Carlo**, Rua dos Murcas 19, and **Rosa d'Ouro**, Rua de António José d'Almeida.

Tapestry

The craft of sewing pictures on canvas was introduced to Madeira by the German artist, Herbert Kiekeben, in 1938. The **Kiekeben** shop, at Rua da Carreira 194, sells wallhangings, chair covers, handbags and carpets, while do-it-yourself tapestry kits can be bought in **Madeira Sun**, Avenida Zarco 4.

Wickerwork

The heart of wicker production is at Camacha (page 80) and although some wickerwork can be purchased throughout the island it is to this village that the visitor should head for the complete range of products and demonstrations of the craftsmen at work. (See also page 82) However, if Camacha is not on your itinerary there is a well-stocked shop in Funchal, at Rua da Carreira 102.

Wines and liqueurs

Many Madeiran souvenir shops sell miniatures and full bottles of non-vintage Madeira, but serious wine lovers should visit Funchal's various wine lodges – the best known is the **Adegas de São Francisco** (page 28) which has a tasting bar and a well-stocked shop, but you should also visit **D'Oliveiras**, at Rua dos Ferreiros 107, an old wine lodge full of dark timbers and delicious smells, or its near neighbour, **Henriques & Henriques**, at Rua dos Ferreiros 125, whose central courtyard is shaded by rampant vines.

Visit the Casa Turistica for the best choice of souvenirs and ceramics

Entertainment

*E*ntertainment on Madeira revolves principally around five-star hotels, such as the Savoy, Casino Park and Carlton. Their shows, dinner dances and folklore evenings are widely advertised. They are open to everyone, including non-residents, and can be booked through any travel agent.

Casino Park Hotel
The Casino Park Hotel mounts three shows a week: *New York, New York* (Fridays) features songs and routines from popular Broadway musicals, *A Night of Romance in Vienna* (Tuesdays), includes ballet performances by local schoolchildren and *Paris je t'aime* (Sundays) features the can-can. Prices include a four-course meal and free entrance after the show to the casino and the Baccara disco.
Quinta da Vigia (tel: 233111).

Madeira Carlton
Folklore and dance feature on the *Madeira Night* programme (Mondays). *Classic Evergreens* (Thursday) features children's ballet and a string quartet playing popular tunes by composers such

Roulette at the Casino Park Hotel

as Strauss, Vivaldi and Mozart, while *Paris Champagne* (Saturday) is a French-style cabaret.
Largo António Nobre (tel: 231031).

Savoy
The Savoy Hotel's regular *This is Madeira* show provides the opportunity to watch the island's traditional song and dance (see page 150) and talk to the performers about their costumes and instruments. Tea dances, jazz nights and big band music also feature on the hotel's schedule.
Avenida do Infante (tel: 222031).

CASINO
The Madeira Casino
Located in the grounds of the Casino Park Hotel, the Casino da Madeira (tel: 231121) offers you the opportunity to throw large sums of money away playing roulette, blackjack or slot machines. The Casino is open from 5pm to 3am to people over 21 years of age. You must show your passport to gain entry and men are expected to wear a jacket and tie.

CINEMA
Popular blockbuster films are shown in the original language (usually American) with Portuguese subtitles at several cinemas in Funchal – their schedules are published daily in the free *Notícias da Madeira* newspaper, available at hotels. Look out too for screenings of more serious films at the **Teatro Municipal**,

Modern cabaret (above) and traditional Portuguese *fado* (right)

on Avenida Arriaga, opposite the Tourist Information Office.

DISCOTHÈQUES

The most popular are **O Farol**, in the Madeira Carlton (tel: 231031) and **Baccara** in the Casino Park Hotel (tel: 231121). The best for local atmosphere is the harbourside disco called **Vespas** on Avenida Sá Carneiro, (open daily from 11pm to 4am). Less formal than the hotel discos is the **Disco Pub Formula 1**, Rua do Favilha 5 (tel: 65755), which is open daily from 9pm to 4am.

FADO

It is difficult to account for the enormous popularity of *fado* (meaning 'fate'), the plaintive Portuguese music and song that tells of tragic events, dark destinies and lost loves, yet popular it is, and there are plenty of opportunities to wallow in an

evening of soulful fatalism. Madeirans themselves rate very highly the performances at the **O Pitéu Bar and Restaurant** (Tuesday, Friday and Saturday), Rua da Carreira 182A (tel: 220819). Equally atmospheric are the **Marcelino Fado House**, Travessa da Torre 22A, in the Zona Velha (Old Town), open daily from 10.30pm to 4am (tel: 230834), and the nearby **Arsenio's Restaurant**, Rua de Santa Maria 169, open daily from noon until 2am (tel: 224007).

MUSIC

Madeira's traditional music and dance makes light of the heavy burdens of work and slavery. In one very distinctive dance the participants turn in slow circles with their heads bowed, taking short steps as if their feet were chained together. It is called the Dance of Ponta do Sol, named after the area where Moorish and African slaves were kept during the early days of the island's colonisation. Similar in style are the Carrier's Dance, representing heavily laden peasants jogging along the island's footpaths beneath stacks of sugarcane or baskets loaded with bananas, and the Heavy Dance, in which the regular rhythmic stamping is said to reflect the custom of crushing grapes to make Madeira wine with the bare feet. Madeiran song is more lighthearted and tells of courtship, the pleasures of the autumn harvest and the joys of wine. By contrast the *charamba* is a kind of musical duel, with a lively chorus, in which two singers improvise alternative verses which satirise the

AND DANCE

other person's looks, character or reputation to the amusement of the audience. Musical accompaniment to both song and dance is provided by the four-stringed *braguinha*, similar to a ukulele, wooden castanets, called *castanholas* and a notched stick called a *raspadeira*, decorated with a carved head and played like a washboard.

Most intriguing of all is the percussive *brinquinho*, a hand-held pole where dolls in Madeiran costume wearing bells and castanets slide up and down to the music. Madeira still has numerous folklore groups who perform at festivals all round the island, dedicated to keeping Madeira's traditions alive. They can also be seen at folklore evenings hosted by Funchal's major hotels and at the **Café Relogio** restaurant in Camacha most evenings (tel: 922114).

The Madeiran song and dance traditions are handed down by each generation

Festivals

*A*lmost every day seems to be a festival day on Madeira – festivals are still announced in the traditional way, by setting off a string of loud explosive fire-crackers and shooting rockets into the air. In the days before telephone, post or newspapers, this was an effective way of sending a message to your neighbours inviting them to come across and join in the fun.

Most village festivals (called *arraiais*) are rooted in the Catholic religion and are held to honour the local patron saint or to celebrate a major event in the church calendar – the Feast of the Assumption (15 August) is one of the biggest, and local celebrations often begin a full fortnight in advance of the day itself. The day will begin with Mass and processions of children and villagers in their best clothes singing hymns. The parish priest, or perhaps the bishop of Funchal, will preach a long sermon about the perils of drinking and dissipation, but by nightfall everyone (including the priest) will be dancing and singing beneath trees illuminated with coloured bulbs, the band on the makeshift stage alternating between Madeiran folk songs and the latest pop chart hits. For visitors, such festivals offer the chance of sampling local wine and *espetada* kebabs cooked the way they should be, over the embers of a vinewood fire.

Other festivals and events are more formal and, with one eye to tourism, have been elaborated in recent years to increase their appeal to visitors. Here is a list of the main events to look out for:

February
Carnival is celebrated in villages all over the island but the costumed parades held in Funchal are the best. The parade held on the Saturday before Shrove Tuesday features satirical floats poking mild fun at the authorities accompanied by bands and fireworks, while a second parade on Shrove Tuesday itself features clowns and fancy dress.

April/May
Madeira's Flower Festival, held on a weekend at the end of April or early in May, sees Funchal transformed into a

The Virgin is honoured throughout Madeira at Assumption (15 August)

blaze of colour. Streets, houses, shop windows and churches are decorated with ribbons, flags, floral carpets and pictures made of flowers. The climax is a parade of flower-smothered floats through the city's main streets.

May/June

Madeira's Music Festival, at the end of May and beginning of June, is a chance to hear students of the local conservatoire perform, as well as guest musicians from around the world. Most of the concerts are held in the cathedral and the elegant Teatro Municipal.

August

Car fanatics regard the Madeira Wine Rally as one of the toughest stages of the European championships and celebrities from all over Europe pour in for the event. If you are in Funchal for the start of the rally in early August you will hear the ear-ripping sound of the rally-car engines but the best way to follow the action is by watching it on TV. Madeira's biggest religious festival takes place on 15 August, when devout Catholics from all over the island come to Our Lady's church at Monte (see page 91), climbing the steps to the church on their knees, to honour the Assumption of the Virgin.

September

Wine festivals held in Funchal and Câmara de Lobos feature wine tasting, dancing in the streets and demonstrations of grape treading (see page 78).

December

Christmas preparations begin as early as 8 December when *bolo do mel* (honey cake) is traditionally made and when

children plant wheat, maize or barley seeds in small pots. About 10 days later the pots begin to sprout a head of fresh green shoots, symbolising renewal and plenty in the year ahead. The pots are placed round the crib figures which are found not just in churches, but also in shop windows, village squares, hotel foyers, restaurants and private homes. From the 8 December Funchal's streets are lit up nightly with coloured bulbs and illuminations, in preparation for the island's spectacular New Year's Eve festival (see page 154).

Brazilian-style costumes and loud samba music are the hallmark of the Funchal Carnival

NEW YEAR

New Year on Madeira is the climax of the island's festive calendar. From the 8 December, the city of Funchal will have been ablaze every night with nearly half a million coloured bulbs, outlining the shapes of buildings, draped over trees and illuminating the waterfront promenade. As New Year approaches, Madeiran emigrants from South America, Australia, Canada and southern Africa fly home to be with their families, joining the hundreds of tourists who jet in to enjoy the warmth of a Madeiran Christmas, and the many sea voyagers – in small boats and in huge luxury liners, such as the *Queen Elizabeth II* and the *Canberra* – who all set sail for Funchal's harbour.

On New Year's Eve itself another migration begins, as Madeirans from all over the island head for Funchal in cars, trucks and buses, clogging up all the approach roads. The aim of all this movement is to be in Funchal for one of the world's most spectacular fireworks displays. As midnight approaches on New Year's Eve, the lights are turned on in every building in Funchal and its suburbs, doors are opened and curtains drawn, so that the whole amphitheatre of hills enclosing the city seems a blaze of lights, matched by the lights of the ships and boats in the harbour. Silence falls, and then, as the bewitching hour strikes, all Funchal explodes with the sound of ship's sirens, the popping of champagne corks, church bells ringing and the cheers of onlookers, all accompanied by a meteor storm of coloured rockets bursting overhead. Those who have seen it once regularly

return,
which is why hotel rates double
over the Christmas and New Year
period – if you want to be there
yourself, be certain to book at least a
year in advance.

Champagne corks and fireworks all reach for
the sky at midnight on New Year

Children

*A*s a destination, Madeira tends to attract older visitors rather than young families and there are fewer facilities for children than you would find in other Portuguese resorts, such as the Algarve. If you do bring your children, though, you can be sure of a warm reception wherever you go because the Madeirans themselves are very indulgent towards the young.

If your children swim and are old enough to be trusted on their own, they will happily spend hours at the pool. The **Lido Complex** (see page 158), located in the Hotel Zone on Rua do Gorgulho, is by far the best pool on Madeira and is preferable to the handkerchief-sized pools that most hotels squeeze on to their terraces or rooftops. The drawback is that it is packed with people at the weekend, so the best time to take your children is during the week. By contrast,

several of the larger hotels have sports facilities that are underused – your children could be encouraged to spend a few hours on the courts improving their tennis, enjoying a few rounds of crazy golf or bashing hell out of a table-tennis ball.

Of the museums in Funchal, the **Museu Municipal** (page 52) will

Many hotels offer a small paddling pool for children as an alternative to the main pool energy in the small playground in the **Jardim de Santa Catarina** park which has swings and climbing frames – though they will probably derive just as much fun from watching the antics of the scurrying wall lizards, or chasing the large butterflies with their tissue-paper wings.

Walking by the seafront is another way to spend some time. There are always boats to see in Funchal's yachting marina, and sometimes huge ocean-going cruisers, as well as working ships stacked with containers. The waters of the marina are surprisingly clean and clear and you can watch shoals of silvery fish, some quite large, darting and turning in the sun-warmed waters.

Playing in the park: a chance for children to make new friends

probably prove the most appealing, both for the stuffed sharks and other monsters of the deep upstairs, and for the real live fish, crabs and lobsters in the small downstairs aquarium. Gorgeously coloured tropical birds can be seen at the **Jardim dos Loiros** (page 42) and there is a small 'zoo' in the public gardens in Santo da Serra, featuring deer, birds of prey and a kangaroo. Neither of these will absorb your children's attention for very long, however, and those who are attuned to environmental issues may well be repelled by the conditions the animals and birds are kept in.

Younger children can burn off some

Come night-time, your children might enjoy some of the shows put on by the hotels, though these are mostly aimed at an older audience. If all else fails, there is always the television – MTV, the music channel, can be relied upon for non-stop pop videos.

Sport

Quite a number of Madeira's visitors come with the idea of getting some gentle exercise and keeping fit, so the better hotels all have pools and tennis courts. The island now has two golf courses, both in spectacular settings, and though it lacks beaches, there is plenty of scope for water sports, including scuba-diving and fishing (see page 133).

Hotel facilities

If sport is a priority, it is worth choosing your hotel on the basis of the facilities it offers. The five-star seafront hotels, such as the Savoy, Madeira Palácio, Carlton, Reid's and Casino Park, all have tennis courts and swimming pools big enough for serious length work. The **Savoy** (tel: 222031) has the best seafront complex of all the hotels, with facilities for windsurfing, sailing, scuba-diving and sea-canoeing as well as a fitness centre and tennis courts. The **Casino Park** (tel: 233111) has the best fitness centre, including a gym, sauna, massage and whirlpool bath.

Guests are given priority when it comes to booking and using the facilities but most hotels admit non-residents on payment of a small admission fee, and this is sometimes waived altogether if you take lunch in the hotel restaurant – enquire when you book your table.

The Lido Complex

For serious swimmers and for families with children the Municipal Lido Complex, on Rua do Gorgulho, offers a good alternative to hotel facilities. The complex includes an Olympic-size pool, children's pool, access to the sea from a diving platform, solariums and several cafés and restaurants. Open daily from 8.30am to 7pm in summer, and 9am to 6pm in winter, the Lido is well worth visiting during the week, but with 3,000 visitors packed into the complex at weekends, it can seem unbearably overcrowded.

Quinta do Magnólia

The island's other public facility is the elegant Quinta do Magnólia (tel: 764598) entered from Rua Dr Pita, next to the Quinta do Sol complex. Built as the British Country Club, the complex now belongs to the Madeiran regional government and the former clubhouse now serves as Madeira's Hotel and

Tennis at the Quinta do Magnólia (left) and the Santo da Serra golf course (right)

Tourism School (see page 162). Within the grounds are tennis and squash courts, a large swimming pool, a putting course and a jogging track. Bookings can be made at the gatekeeper's lodge at the park entrance, open daily from 8am to 9pm.

Golf

Madeira has two golf courses, both noted for their magnificent views and picturesque setting. The older one is the 27-hole, 6,015m, **Santo da Serra** course (tel: 552345) set high on a plateau to the east of the island, venue for the Madeira Open tournament (held every January) which attracts many top international players. The newer course is the 18-hole, 6,015m, **Palheiro Golf** (tel: 792116), situated high above Funchal and carved out of the 324-hectare Quinta do Palheiro estate. The views are enhanced by the surrounding woodland, much of it planted by the Blandy family since they acquired the estate in 1885 (see page 104).

Horse riding

Contact the Centro de Hipismo da Madeira, Caminho dos Pretos (tel: 224982) which is open Monday to Friday, 9.30am to 5pm. Bookings can also be made through the nearby Hotel Estrelícia on Caminho Velho da Ajuda (tel: 230131).

Football

Madeirans are passionate about football and claim that the game was introduced to Portugal via Madeira – quite likely, given the island's long-standing relationship with Britain. The Estádio dos Barreiros stadium, whose concrete bulk looms just north of the Hotel Zone is home to Madeira's first division team, C S Marítimo, which plays on alternate Sunday afternoons in the season. Football is a family affair and there is no risk of violence. The stadium stands high above Funchal so, as the locals say, if there is not much happening on the field, you can always enjoy the view.

Food and Drink

You can eat out of doors almost all the year round on Madeira, because of the island's mild climate, and most restaurants spill out on to the pavement, or have rooftop terraces, so that you can make the most of the chance to dine beneath the stars. The food itself is fresh, wholesome and inexpensive – the only drawback is the lack of variety since the menus of most Madeiran restaurants scarcely differ in any respect other than price.

Ambience and location therefore count for a great deal when you decide where to dine, and there are several distinct restaurant areas in Funchal. The Hotel Zone is well supplied, and it is here that you will find the greatest choice, from the international *haute cuisine* of the five-star hotel grill rooms, to the several Chinese, Indian and Italian restaurants that offer a break from a diet of Madeiran kebabs or grilled sardines.

If you are a seafood fanatic, then the restaurants lining Funchal's yacht marina are the best bet – here you can select crabs or lobsters live from the tank, or choose from a vast range of shellfish or grilled fresh fish and look out on to the mast-filled marina while you eat. Further east, many of the pavement cafés of the Zona Velha (Old Town) offer the cheapest prices in Funchal and a festive, youthful atmosphere, especially at weekends in summer when some cafés

Novelty dining at Funchal's harbourside floating restaurant complex

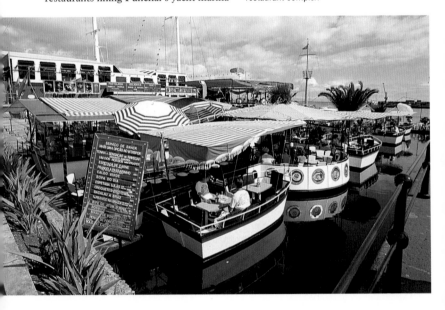

lay on musical entertainment and the party goes on well into the night.

Prices

It is easy to eat well and cheaply on Madeira if you eat local food and drink local wines. The prices begin to rise as soon as you go for anything imported. Don't forget, too, that some dishes, especially seafood and fish, are priced according to weight and by the prevailing market price – before you order an expensive out-of-season fish, be sure to ask the waiter for an idea of what a portion will cost.

Whatever dish you order will automatically be served with salad and potatoes, so you do not need to order any side dishes, unless you wish. In the restaurant listings below, the following symbols have been used to indicate the approximate cost per person of a two-course meal with alcohol and a coffee:

$ = Up to 1,500$
$$ = 1,500$–2,000$
$$$ = 2,000$–3,750$
$$$$ = More than 3,750$

RESTAURANTS

HOTEL ZONE
A Rampa $$
Excellent seafood salads, pizzas and homemade pasta, but the outdoor dining terrace suffers from overlooking a busy road.
Henry II Building (opposite Savoy Hotel), 1st Floor, Avenida do Infante (tel: 35275).

Bamboo Inn $$$
Smart and efficient Chinese restaurant.
Estrada Monumental 318, 2nd Floor (tel: 226861).

Bombay Palace $$$
Typical tandoori restaurant plus all kinds of curry.
Eden Mar Shopping Center, Rua do Gorgulho (tel: 763110).

Casa Velha $$$
Elegant dining in a well-restored 19th-century town house; specialises in *flambé* dishes and lobster with pasta.
Rua Imperatriz Dona Amélia 69 (tel: 225749).

Casa dos Reis $$$
Intimate restaurant behind the Savoy Hotel serving French and international cuisine.
Rua da Penha de França 6 (tel: 225182).

Doca do Cavacas $$
Atmospheric restaurant specialising in seafood and fresh fish.
Ponta da Cruz, Estrada Monumental (tel: 762057).

Dona Amélia $$$$
Elegant but pricey international standard cuisine, set in a restored 19th-century town house with intimate terrace.
Rua Imperatriz Dona Amélia 83 (tel: 225784).

Don Filet $$$
Brazilian-style charcoal-grilled beef plus local *espetada* kebabs and piano music.
Rua do Favila 7, by the Savoy Hotel (tel: 764426).

Fleur-de-Lys $$$$
The Savoy Hotel's flagship restaurant; top quality international cuisine, impeccable service and panoramic views over Funchal and the harbour. Reservations essential.
Savoy Hotel, Avenida do Infante (tel: 222031).

Hong Kong $$

Authentic Cantonese food and décor.
*Olimpo Shopping Centre, Avenida do
Infante (tel: 228181).*

Kon Tiki $$$

The owner of this lively restaurant likes
to greet arriving guests. The eclectic
menu features tuna, shark, charcoal-
grilled beef and *espada flambé* with
prawns.
*Rua do Favila 9, by the Savoy Hotel (tel:
764737).*

Les Faunes $$$$

Probably Madeira's best restaurant, the
haunt of visiting dignitaries and those
who can afford a very special night out.
Formal evening dress is not compulsory
but is worn by most of the guests.
Reservations advised.
*Reid's Hotel, Estrada Monumental (tel:
766466).*

Moby Dick $$

Fish restaurant specialising in *espada de
camarão* (scabbard fish with shrimps)
and *atum con todos* (literally 'tuna with
everything').
Estrada Monumental 187 (tel: 66868).

Quinta do Magnólia $$$

The former British Country Club now
houses the Escola de Hotelaria e
Turismo (Hotel and Tourism School)
whose graduates often go on to work in
top hotels and restaurants all over
Europe. The main building has now
been turned into an elegant dining room
with terrace where you can enjoy an
excellent and inexpensive four-course
meal, with several choices for each
course, while being waited upon by the
school's advanced-level students. The
only drawback is that it only serves
lunch and not dinner, though afternoon
tea is also available, with home-made
cakes (4pm–7pm) and you can make use
of the swimming pool and tennis courts
in the grounds (see Sport, page 158).
The bar opens at noon and lunch is
served from 1pm.
*Booking, at least one day in advance, is
essential. Dress casual but smart. Closed
Sunday.*
Rua do Dr Pita (tel: 764013).

Reid's Dining Room $$$$

Slightly less expensive than Les Faunes,
but equally smart (evening dress
advised), Reid's main dining room offers
chandeliered elegance and a choice of
reasonably priced set menus or more
highly priced *á la carte*. Dinner only.
Reservations advised.
*Reid's Hotel, Estrada Monumental (tel:
766466).*

Packed with choice, the Old Town (right)

Sol e Mar $$

Lively and informal good value
restaurant offering pizza, pasta, *flambé* or
Madeiran dishes, including the excellent
fish stew.
*Flor do Lido Building, Estrada
Monumental 314-B (tel: 762030).*

DOWNTOWN FUNCHAL
A Flor $$

Typically Madeiran but with a more
expensive menu than most and
impeccable service.
Rua da Queimada de Baixo 3 (tel: 36284).

Arsénio's $$

Pizza and fish restaurant in the Old
Town popular for its live *fado* singing
and music.
Rua de Santa Maria 169 (tel: 224007).

Café Esplenada Arco-Velho $

The best of a run of pavement cafés in
the Old Town. Friendly service and a
good choice of authentic local dishes, at
rock-bottom prices.
Rua de Carlos I, 42 (no telephone).

Caravelha $$$

Smart *flambé* restaurant with harbour
views and one of the few in Madeira to
offer a specific vegetarian menu. Seafood
risotto (*arroz de mariscos*) is also a
popular choice.
Avenida do Mar 15 (tel: 228464).

Carochinha $$$

Everything about this restaurant is
reminiscent of English Sunday lunch –
except that Sunday is the one day it is
closed! Lunch on roast beef and apple

Nautical décor promising fresh fish

crumble or enjoy smoked salmon and mixed grill by candlelight.
Rua do São Francisco 2A (tel: 223695).

O Celeiro $$$
Smart cellar restaurant, ideal for a romantic candle-lit dinner, serving grilled fish, seafood and typical Madeiran dishes.
Rua dos Aranhas 22 (tel: 230622).

Fim de Século $$
The friendly and intimate 'End of the Century' restaurant has a certain Victorian air to the décor and serves healthy portions of garlic prawns or grilled tuna washed down with jugs of sangria.
Rua da Carreira 144 (tel: 224476).

Golfinho $$
Old Town restaurant with nautical décor specialising in fresh seafood but also serving good value beef and chicken dishes.
Largo do Corpo Santo, 21 (tel: 226774).

O Jango $
A tiny Old Town restaurant which only seats 20 customers, so booking is advised. It specialises in *arroz de mariscos* (seafood rice).
Rua de Santa Maria 166 (tel: 221280).

Le Jardin $$
Old Town restaurant specialising in *flambé* fish or peppered steak.
Rua de Carlos I, 60 (tel: 222864).

Londres $$
Authentic Madeiran and mainland

Portuguese cuisine with a different speciality each day of the week – a good place to sample *bacalhau* (salt cod) transformed into a delicious casserole. Closed Sunday.
Rua da Carreira 64A (tel: 35329).

Marina Terrace $$

Pizza, seafood and live entertainment most nights with sea views. One of several good restaurants fronting the yacht marina.
Marina do Funchal (tel: 34546).

Marisa $

Another good choice for seafood in the Old Town. Try the *lulas grelhadas* (grilled squid) as a change from Madeiran *espetada* kebabs.
Rua de Santa Maria 152 (no telephone).

Pavement cafés abound on the island, with views of the street or out to sea

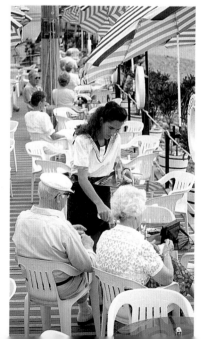

Solar da Santola $$

Another seafront restaurant specialising in fish. The nearly adjacent Papa Massa restaurant belongs to the same chain and serves excellent pizza and pasta at good value prices.
Solar da Santola, Marina do Funchal (tel: 227291); Papa Massa (tel: 37050).

Vagrant $$

Also known as 'The Beatles Boat' because it was once owned by the famous four, this now forms the centrepiece of Funchal's so-called 'Floating Restaurant' area, but do not worry if you suffer from sea sickness – these boats are firmly bedded in concrete and their floating days are well and truly over. Despite the gimmicky ambience, you can eat well here on pizza or typical Madeiran food at reasonable prices.
Avenida do Mar (tel: 223572).

The Madeiran Menu I

*I*t may seem that Madeiran menus are deliberately designed to confuse non-Portuguese visitors. Three of the most popular dishes all have very similar names: *espada* (scabbard fish), *espetada* (beef kebabs) and *espadarte* (swordfish). Learn the difference between these three and you will have the key to eating well during your stay.

Espada

Espada are the rather ugly-looking elongated fish that you will see for sale in the Mercado dos Lavradores (Workers' Market) in Funchal. The name *espada* means scabbard, referring to their long flat shape. Once cleaned and prepared for cooking they look innocuous enough, but in the market their long snout, vicious teeth and over-large eyes are the stuff of nightmares.

In fact, *espada* are very unusual fish, unique to the waters around Madeira and to certain islands in Japan. They live at very great depths – below 800m, hence their large eyes, necessary for seeing in the gloom. They are carnivorous, hence the razor-sharp teeth, and they rise to 500m at night to feed, which is when Madeira's fishermen make their catch, using long lines with up to 150 hooks baited with squid. Decompression kills the fish before they reach the surface and their meat is very versatile: in authentic Madeiran

restaurants it is likely to be served *com banana* (fried in butter with a slice of banana on top) or *com vinho e alhos* (marinaded in wine and vinegar before frying in olive oil); in tourist restaurants it is more likely to be served with white wine sauce and prawns.

Espetada

Espetada consists of chunks of beef, skewered on a stick made from the fresh green wood of the bay tree, which imparts flavour to the meat as it cooks. The meat is rolled in chopped garlic, sea salt and crushed bay leaves and traditionally the kebabs are grilled over the embers of a fire made from vine prunings, which adds another subtle layer of flavouring. This dish, once reserved for special festivities, such as Christmas and the Feast of the Assumption, is now the staple of Madeiran restaurant menus, where it is often cooked under an electric grill and thus lacks the genuine taste of wood-cooked meat. At some rural restaurants, such as the **Abrigo do Poiso** (tel: 782259), located at Poiso (see page 98) on the road between Funchal and Faial, you can watch *espetada* being cooked the traditional way, on an open fire, and savour the difference. To accompany the meat, chips and salad are usually served, and in traditional restaurants chunks of

Espada: ugly but delicious

Espetada: traditionally grilled over the scented wood of vines or bay trees

bolo de caco. This country bread is made from nothing but flour, sweet potatoes, a small amount of yeast and water; allowed to prove for 24 hours, it is then shaped into flat circles and cooked quickly on top of a flat stone heated in the same open fire used to cook the kebabs. The result is a spongy open-textured bread with a delicious crust.

Espadarte and other fish

Espadarte, or swordfish, is one of several big and meaty fish that you will find on the menu in restaurants specialising in fish and seafood. Others include *pargo* (bream), *salmonete* (red mullet) and *atum* (tuna), usually served grilled with onion sauce and accompanied by *milho frito*, deep-fried cubes of maize flour mixed with cabbage and herbs.

Nearly all fish restaurants serve seafood paella (*arroz de mariscos*) because it is such a spectacular dish, garlanded with prawns and decked with all kinds of shellfish, but the dish and its ingredients are imported for the sake of visitors and likely to be expensive. If you want to go native, then try *bacalhau a Gomes de Sá* (salt cod casseroled with onions, potatoes, garlic and olives, and garnished with chopped boiled eggs) or *caldeirada*, a tasty fish stew made from fish, potatoes, onions and tomatoes.

The seafood gourmet's delight

The Madeiran Menu II

*A*s soon as you are seated at any good Madeiran café or restaurant table, the waiter is likely to present you with a plate of warm bread, dripping with garlic butter. Hoping that the garlic will counterbalance the cholesterol effects of the butter, you can enjoy this deliciously simple food while pondering the menu.

Starters

The most typical Madeiran starters are grilled limpets and tomato soup. With limpets (*lapas*) you risk pushing the cholesterol count even higher, since they are often served in the shell in a puddle of melted garlic butter, but these are the only native Madeiran shellfish – everything else is imported. Healthier by far is *sopa de tomate* made from finely chopped onions and tomatoes with a lightly poached egg added to each person's bowl before serving.

Grilled limpets in garlic-flavoured butter

Main courses and side dishes

All main courses (see page 167) come with potatoes (boiled with fish, chips with meat) and salad or vegetables, so you do not need to order any side dishes unless you wish – if you do, make it clear you want the side dish served at the same time as the main course, otherwise it will be presented on its own, after the starter.

Desserts

Rarely will you be offered much of a choice. Ice cream is ubiquitous but you may be offered fruit salad – if this is fresh it can be delicious, incorporating the best of the island's tropical varieties, such as papaya, passion fruit, mangoes and custard apples.

Drinks

Coral beer is brewed on Madeira and is a light refreshing lager with a flowery fragrance. Ask for it by name, or else you are likely to be served San Miguel or some other beer imported from the mainland. Madeiran table wine is also very drinkable, but it is hard to find in Funchal, despite laws requiring bars and restaurants to offer it on their wine lists. Restaurateurs make more money from selling expensive imported wines; if you ask for local wine you are quite likely to be told 'it's not very nice'. In reality the local wine is light, refreshing, only just fermented, and as much like grape juice in character as wine. Look out for what the locals drink. Among imported wines, chilled and slightly sparkling *Vinho Verde* (young or 'green' wine) is a reliable choice to accompany fish and the robust oaky reds from Dão and Bairrada reveal their rich character when drunk with meat. Coffee on Madeira is continental in style – you will be served an *espresso* (*bica* in Portuguese) unless you request otherwise. With it you might like to try one of the island's numerous liqueurs – *maracujá* (made from passion fruit) is said to be an excellent aphrodisiac, and equally palatable is *ginja* (made from cherries) and *licor de castanha* (distilled from sweet chestnuts).

Snacks

Madeira's staple lunchtime sandwich is the *prego no prato*, made from country bread spread with garlic butter and enclosing a chunk of grilled steak – a robust and filling energy-reviver served in traditional bars or cafés. Vegetarians have a harder time, but new-style cafés, such as Vivaldi (Rua da Figueira Preta 6; tel: 222028, just off Rua 31 de Janeiro) are beginning to appear offering delicatessen-style salads and gourmet sandwiches, plus very good home-made ice cream. Another staple is *bolo do mel* (honey cake), sold in every *pastelaria* (baker's shop). Traditionally made at Christmas,

Sugar-cane spirit, drink with lemon and honey

but consumed all year, this dark, fruit-filled, spicey cake contains many ingredients – but honey is not one of them; the sweetness comes from the hot molasses added to the cake dough before it is cooked, a legacy of Madeira's ancient sugar-cane industry.

Dark and spice-rich *bolo de mel* (honey cake)

Hotels and Accommodation

*M*adeira has a wide choice of good-quality accommodation, ranging from venerable old hotels such as Reid's (see page 172) down to inexpensive self-catering apartments. Package holiday prices are hard to beat but you must book well in advance if you want to visit during the school holiday periods, remembering that Madeira is as popular in winter as in summer – in fact Christmas and New Year are the most expensive times to visit because of the festivities (see page 154).

If you do book a package to Madeira, be sure to compare operators' prices because they vary quite a lot, even for identical rooms in the same hotel. Be careful, too, to check how far out of town the hotel is situated – some are up to 5km from the city centre, and though they offer a shuttle bus service, you will still feel isolated. On the other hand, these hotels are often cheaper to stay in. Price bands (per double room without sea view):

Luxury hotels £75–£100 per night
Standard hotels £35–£50 per night
Pensions £15–£30 per night
Rates vary markedly according to the season.

Five-star hotels

You cannot go wrong if you choose to stay in one of Funchal's five-star hotels. All of them occupy prime positions in

THOMAS COOK
Traveller's Tip

Anyone who purchases travel tickets from any Thomas Cook network location is entitled to use the services of any other Thomas Cook network location, free of charge, to make hotel reservations.

the Hotel Zone, less than ten minutes' walk from the city centre, with splendid sea views, huge swimming pools and direct access to the sea, with roped-off bathing areas. You will be charged a supplement for a room with a sea view but you may consider this worthwhile since rooms without sea views look on to the busy Estrada Monumental.

Three- and four-star hotels

Most of the island's hotels fall into this category and are located in the sprawl of high-rise developments stretching westwards from the city centre along the Estrada Monumental.

Nearly all the hotels have a pool, but rarely big enough for serious swimming, though the excellent Lido pool complex (see Sport, page 158) is located in the midst of the Hotel Zone, and the area is well supplied with shops and restaurants. Nearly all the hotels are modern, and you can usually count on your own balcony and bathroom, satellite TV, direct-dial telephones plus a café, bar and small shop. Breakfast is nearly always included in the room price – this can range from tea or coffee, a bread roll and fruit to a sumptuous buffet spread.

Quinta-style hotels

Many elegant *quintas* (or mansions) were demolished to make way for the high-

Five-star luxury: Madeira's best hotels all have large seafront swimming pools

rises of the Hotel Zone but thankfully others have survived and a few have been converted into elegant, antique-filled hotels set in well-tended gardens – worth seeking out if you are an incurable romantic with a pocket to match.

Self-catering

Funchal has many inexpensive apartments and aparthotels where the accommodation includes a small kitchen and a living/eating area – excellent if you want to take children or prepare your own meals. Private apartments with maid service are also available; look for classified advertisements in the travel sections of the weekend newspapers.

Budget accommodation

No-frills accommodation is available in *pensãos* (pensions), often located above shops, bars or restaurants. The setting is not always tranquil, but the prices are very reasonable, and ideal for young people travelling on a tight budget.

Beyond Funchal

Several towns along Madeira's southern coast have resort complexes, with a mix of hotels and apartments, which some visitors use as an alternative base for exploring the island, especially those who want to escape from the city and enjoy relative solitude. The island also has two *pousadas*, state-owned hotels, deliberately sited in isolated positions and popular with walkers. The 18-room Pousada do Pico do Arieiro (tel: 230110) is located at the summit of Madeira's third highest peak and is perfect for those who want to experience the silence of the mountains, the beauty of the night sky and the glowing light of the rising sun. The other hotel is the Pousada dos Vinháticos, at Serra da Água (tel: 952148). Both need booking several days in advance, longer if you want to stay at the weekend.

REID'S HOTEL

Reid's is one of those legendary hotels which nearly everyone has heard of, the sort of place which regularly entertains Hollywood film stars, royalty and heads of state. In rags-to-riches fashion, the hotel was founded by William Reid, one of twelve children of an impoverished Scottish crofter. Reid set off in 1836 to make his fortune, and worked his passage on board ship to Madeira where he met William Wilkinson. Together they set up an agency catering to the needs of Madeira's wealthy foreign visitors, most of whom would hire a *quinta* (a large house and garden) for the duration of their stay, relying on Reid to find a suitable property and furnish it according to their tastes. The money Reid made enabled him to buy *quintas* and convert them into residential hotels; eventually he bought the plot of land on which Reid's Hotel now sits, enjoying a prime clifftop position with wonderful sea views.

William Reid did not live to see his dream fulfilled – he died in 1888 aged 66, while the hotel was under construction – but his sons took over and opened the doors of this luxury

Reid's is proud of its traditional values

Tea on the balcony (above) with an unrivalled view; luxury cruise passengers arrive by boat at the hotel's private landing stage (right) and are carried by lift up the cliffs to their rooms hotel to the first paying guests in 1891. British Prime Minister Winston Churchill was just one of the many regular guests who would arrive by sea, at the hotel's private landing stage, to be carried by lift to the upper gardens, immaculately tended and filled with palms. The hotel buildings resemble a cross between a colonial gentlemen's club and an aristocrat's home. Even if you cannot afford to stay at Reid's, you can still enjoy the hushed ambience and impeccable service by splashing out on afternoon tea (Madeira cake and cucumber sandwiches with the crusts removed). The poolside buffet lunch is another way of taking in the hotel's style, or you can sip Madeira in the cocktail bar. Just remember to dress smartly, though, or you might be politely turned away – the hotel no longer insists that evening dress be worn for dinner, but it does suggest that you might feel conspicuous if you do not.

On Business

*T*ourism remains Madeira's principal income earner, with wine, flowers, fruit, embroidery and basketry as the principal exports. These are relatively mature industries, with little scope for growth in the future, although tourism still offers plenty of opportunities for small entrepreneurs to enter the market and offer new services.

Recognising the need to diversify, the Madeiran government has set up the Zona Franca Industrial, a duty-free industrial zone, in the east of the island, near Caniçal. The idea is that manufacturers should be able to import raw materials and export finished goods without paying any taxes and levies, but the project is in its infancy and is relatively small-scale.

Madeira also has quite a sophisticated banking system, thanks to the large number of so-called 'emigrants', who leave the island to work abroad, but who remit their foreign currency earnings home, or who return to Madeira after a number of years with a substantial nest

egg. This banking expertise, combined with the fact that Madeira is free to make its own fiscal laws, has led some commentators to speculate whether Madeira might not develop into an offshore banking haven for Europe, especially as the future of Far Eastern banking centres – such as Hong Kong and its near neighbour, Portuguese-administered Macao – looks uncertain once they revert to Chinese rule.

Emigrants
The wealth of some Madeiran emigrants is the stuff of island legends. Some made

A potential off-shore banking haven

Post-modernism comes to Madeira: showrooms on the outskirts of Funchal

their fortunes working in oil-rich Venezuela while others built up retail or restaurant businesses in Africa and Asia. One of the best-known examples is Manuel Pestana, who emigrated to South Africa in the 1940s and made his fortune selling beer, wines and spirits. His son, Dionísio Pestana, now heads the Pestana Group, which owns the Madeira Carlton and Casino Park hotels and has major interests in hotels, aviation and real estate.

Business culture

The Pestana family typify the entrepreneurship that characterises most Madeirans, and in theory doing business in Madeira ought to be relatively straightforward. In practice, people who have experience of the Madeiran business culture report that it is very difficult to make headway without the involvement of local Madeiran partners. As a first step, the local Chamber of Commerce provides information and introductions. Contact the Câmara de Comércio e Indústria da Madeira, at Avenida Arriaga 41 (tel: 230137).

Conferences

All the features which make Madeira a good holiday destination also make it a popular place for holding conferences. All of the five-star hotels offer facilities, but the Madeira Carlton and the Casino Park Hotel both have purpose-designed conference centres and host most of the prestigious international trade fairs and conferences. For information contact: the Casino Park Hotel, Quinta da Vigia (tel: 233111); Madeira Carlton, Largo António Nobre (tel: 231031).

Practical Guide

ARRIVING

Passports

The rules for entering Madeira are the same as those for the Portuguese mainland: citizens of other European Union member states and those from the USA, Canada, Australia and New Zealand can stay for up to 60 days without a visa. You will need to show your passport on entry; you will also need it when registering at hotels or changing money and travellers' cheques.

Travellers who require visas should obtain them in their country of residence, as it may prove difficult to obtain them elsewhere. In the UK, the Thomas Cook Passport and Visa Service can advise on and obtain the necessary documentation – consult your Thomas Cook travel consultant.

By Air

The cheapest way to get to Madeira is by chartered flight. Tour operators specialising in Madeira offer direct flights to Funchal as part of a hotel and flight package, but many of them also offer inexpensive flight-only deals using airlines such as the Madeira-based Air Columbia. TAP (Air Portugal), the national carrier, also offers scheduled flights direct to Funchal as well as via Lisbon. These flights are more expensive but you can fly any day of the week and, to compete with the charter carriers, TAP often runs special schemes involving free car rental or the option to stop off in Lisbon at no extra cost.

Airport Facilities

Funchal's Santa Catarina airport is small and efficient, and lies 18km outside the city. You will rarely experience delays except in very severe weather; even this is less of a problem because the runway was upgraded and extended in 1990 allowing much larger planes to use the airport. There is a viewing platform on the roof of the terminal building and all the usual airport facilities: a small duty-free shop, a change bureau and several car hire agencies. Waiters and waitresses will serve you in the airport bars and cafés, though the service can be slow. The airport lets itself down by having some of the most unpleasant toilets on the island.

The airport has no flight information service.

City link

Transport from the airport to your hotel is usually included in package tours. If not, there are taxis available just outside the terminal exit doors and the fare into central Funchal was about 3,500$ in 1994. There is a very cheap bus that calls at the airport at regular intervals throughout the day. The drive to Funchal takes 20–30 minutes by taxi, 60 minutes by bus.

By sea

There are no ferry services to Madeira but British, Russian and Norwegian cruise liners regularly visit the island as part of a week-long tour of the Canary Islands, Madeira and North Africa.

Cruise passengers rarely get more than 24 hours on Madeira, scarcely long enough to sample the island's varied attractions, but some cruise companies allow you to take just part of the cruise, perhaps arriving in Madeira romantically by sea and returning home by air.

CAMPING

Officially there is only one campsite on Madeira, the tiny Parque de Campismo (tel: 852447) located on the seafront at Porto Moniz. Basic camping facilities (water standpipes and barbecue pits) are also provided in many of the island's inland forest parks; you will not have to look far to find them because there will always be a cluster of tents near by. To camp in the parks visitors must first obtain a licence from the forest park guards.

The Madeirans themselves enjoy camping, especially in summer and at weekends. Hardy walkers on Madeira often dispense with a tent altogether and sleep under the stars in a waterproof sleeping bag – in summer it is dry and warm enough to do this and Madeira has no venomous snakes or insects to make this hazardous.

Camping at Porto Moniz

Conversion Table

FROM	TO	MULTIPLY BY
Inches	Centimetres	2.54
Feet	Metres	0.3048
Yards	Metres	0.9144
Miles	Kilometres	1.6090
Acres	Hectares	0.4047
Gallons	Litres	4.5460
Ounces	Grams	28.35
Pounds	Grams	453.6
Pounds	Kilograms	0.4536
Tons	Tonnes	1.0160

To convert back, for example from centimetres to inches, divide by the number in the third column.

Men's Suits

UK		36	38	40	42	44	46	48
Rest of Europe	46	48	50	52	54	56	58
US		36	38	40	42	44	46	48

Dress Sizes

UK		8	10	12	14	16	18
France		36	38	40	42	44	46
Italy		38	40	42	44	46	48
Rest of Europe		34	36	38	40	42	44
US		6	8	10	12	14	16

Men's Shirts

UK	14	14.5	15	15.5	16	16.5	17
Rest of Europe	36	37	38	39/40	41	42	43
US	14	14.5	15	15.5	16	16.5	17

Men's Shoes

UK	7	7.5	8.5		9.5	10.5	11
Rest of Europe	41	42	43		44	45	46
US	8	8.5	9.5		10.5	11.5	12

Women's Shoes

UK	4.5	5	5.5	6	6.5	7
Rest of Europe	38	38	39	39	40	41
US	6	6.5	7	7.5	8	8.5

CHILDREN

For advice on enjoying Madeira with children see pages 156–7.

CLIMATE

Funchal has an almost perfect climate; temperatures do not vary much from an average of 22°C throughout the year, making it a perfect place to escape from the cold of northern European winters or the excessive heat of summer. Funchal and other towns on the south side of the island receive very little rain, except in autumn. The weather on the rest of the island is variable, depending on altitude and aspect with the north receiving most of the rain, and rainclouds hanging almost permanently at the 800–1,000m level (see page 18 for further information).

CRIME

Crime is an evil that has yet to take root in Madeira. Within the island's close-knit communities, still strongly influenced by the teachings of the Roman Catholic church, serious crimes are so as to be profoundly shocking when they do occur. Even so, you should not offer an invitation to crime by being careless with your valuables; use your hotel safe and do not leave possessions in unattended cars. Do report crime at once if you fall a victim – the police will do everything possible to help (see Police, page 186).

CUSTOMS

As Madeira is part of the European Union, visitors from its member countries benefit from new regulations introduced in 1993. The amount of duty-paid goods (those bought in local shops) you can take home from Madeira is only restricted by notional limits, above which you may be asked to prove that your purchases are

FUNCHAL

October–March

April–September

mm
150
125
100
75
50
25
0

°C
30
25
20
15
10
5
0

J F M A M J J A S O N D

WEATHER CONVERSION CHART
25.4mm = 1 inch
°F = 1.8 × °C + 32

for personal rather than commercial use. If you are aged 17 or over you can bring back:
800 cigarettes, 400 cigarillos, 200 cigars, 1kg of tobacco, 90 litres of wine, 10 litres of spirits, 20 litres of fortified wine (or 26 bottles of Madeira), and 100 litres of beer. The allowances for goods bought in duty-free shops (in airports or on board ships and planes), sold free of customs duty and VAT, are unchanged; they also apply to anyone visiting Madeira from a country outside the EU.

The allowances here are (per person aged over 17):
200 cigarettes or 100 cigarillos or 50 cigars or 250 gms of tobacco;
1 litre of spirits or 2 litres of table wine and 2 litres of fortified or sparkling wine; 75 gms of perfume.

These limits may vary from time to time so it is best to check when you make your purchase – current limits are posted in duty-free shops.

DISABLED VISITORS
Facilities for disabled visitors to Madeira are limited. TAP Air Portugal has provision for passengers with wheelchairs, and luxury hotels, such as the Savoy and Madeira Palácio, are able to offer accommodation of an acceptable standard, as can the Luamar Hotel on Porto Santo.

DRIVING
Renting a car gives you the flexibility to explore the island at your own pace. Bear in mind, though, that the daily cost of car hire is about the same as hiring a taxi for the day, with the advantage that the taxi driver takes the strain of the island's steep and tortuous roads. Remember that if you do hire a car, the driver is not going to see much of the countryside,

It is best to fill up petrol tanks before heading off the beaten track

because total concentration is needed to avoid the myriad hazards; these include hairpin bends without crash barriers to prevent you plunging down the mountainsides, roads so narrow that only one car can pass, sheep and humans in the middle of the road, and other drivers (especially over-confident Madeirans overtaking on impossible bends).

Most drivers are courteous and they rarely break the speed limits of 60kph in built-up areas and 90kph elsewhere. Cars drive on the right, seat-belts must be worn and children under 12 are not allowed in the front seats. The more expensive hotels provide covered parking. Public car parks are located beneath the Marina Shopping Centre on Avenida do Mar and on the site of the old bus station near the Zona Velha. You pay by the hour but the cost is reasonable. Outside Funchal free parking places are easy to find. There are plenty of petrol stations in Funchal, including one that is open virtually around the clock on Avenida do Infante, nearly opposite the Casino Park Hotel. It is a good idea to fill your tank before driving to the interior or north of the island where petrol stations are few and far

between. Warning triangles must be used if you break down, positioned in the road to the rear of the car. There are orange SOS call points at regular intervals beside main roads – walk to the nearest, press the button and wait for the rescue service to answer. Alternatively, car rental companies will give you a telephone number that you can use to call out their own rescue service.

Car rental

If you do decide to explore Madeira at your own pace by car, be sure to book well in advance for the peak summer period (July, August and September) and for Christmas and New Year.

Look out too for the special 'Explorer' packages organised by travel agencies, which allow you to tour the island, staying in a different hotel every night, which include the cost of car rental.

To hire a car you must be over 23 years of age with at least a year's driving experience; your own licence is sufficient for driving on Madeira – you do not need an international licence. You will be asked to leave credit card details or a cash deposit.

Atlas, Rua da Alegria 23B (tel: 223100)

Avis, Santa Catarina Airport (tel: 524392)

Brava Car, Caminho do Amparo 2 (tel: 764400)

Hertz, Santa Catarina Airport (tel: 524360)

Insular, Caminho Velhoda Ajuda 27A (tel: 62130)

O Moinho, Estrada Monumental (tel: 762123)

ELECTRICITY

The standard supply on Madeira is 220 volts. Your appliance will work if it is fitted with a two-pin plug; otherwise an adaptor is needed which your hotel can usually supply.

EMBASSIES AND CONSULATES

UK: Blandy Brothers, Avenida Zarco 2, 4th floor (tel: 221221).

USA: Avenida Luis de Comões, Edifício Infante Bloco B, Apartamento B, 4th Floor (tel: 743429).

EMERGENCY TELEPHONE NUMBERS

Hospital: 742111

Fire, Police or Ambulance: 115.

In the event of the loss or theft of your Thomas Cook MasterCard travellers' cheques, tel: 0505 44 9095 (toll-free, 24-hour service) for a refund.

HEALTH

Take care in the sun, whether out walking or by the pool. You can get burned very quickly, as the sun is more intense than you think, despite the relatively low temperatures.

If you do have a health problem you can safely put yourself in the hands of the island's well-trained English-speaking doctors who have a long tradition of helping people who come to Madeira for medical care. The following both have practices close to the Hotel Zone and are used by all the tour operators.

Doctor: Dr Zino, Avenida do Infante 26 (tel: 742227)

Dentist: Dr J Sousa, Infante Shopping Centre (tel: 31277)

If you seek medical treatment remember to keep all bills and receipts in order to claim on your travel insurance policy. Citizens of the European Union can obtain free treatment provided that the relevant documents are obtained before you leave home (in the UK ask for form E111 at post offices). The completed form and your passport must be presented before treatment is sought at the Serviço de Migrantes, Centro do Saúde de Bom Jesus, Rua das Hortas 67 (tel: 229161). Open: Monday to Friday, 9.30am–noon and 2pm–4pm. Outside Funchal, nearly every community has a health centre (*Centro do Saúde*) where help can be sought, and there are emergency services (*urgência*) at the health centres in Ribeira Brava, Calheta, São Vicente, Porto Moniz, Santana, Machico and, on Porto Santo, Vila Baleira.

Madeira has no mandatory vaccination requirements, and no vaccination recommendations other than to keep tetanus and polio immunisation up to date. Like every other part of the world, AIDS is present.

Madeira's food and water are safe. Up-to-date health advice can be obtained from your Thomas Cook travel consultant or direct from the Thomas Cook Travel Clinic, 45 Berkeley Street, London W1A 1EB (tel: 071-408 4157). This is open for consultation without appointment from 8.30am to 5.30pm, Monday to Friday; the staff can give vaccinations, as well as supplying medical advice and a range of first-aid and travel health items.

LANGUAGE

Most Madeirans speak basic English and the staff of shops, hotels and restaurants will be fluent. It is worth knowing some basic Portuguese phrases, however, since you are likely to hear them spoken a lot, and you may even want to try them out yourself. Remember that in Portuguese, the letter s is pronounced like the *s* in sugar unless it is followed by a vowel; thus *carros* (car) is pronounced *carrosh*. The letter *z* sounds similar, so *faz favor* (please) is pronounced *fash favor*. When the tilde accent (~) appears above the letters *ao* (as in *pão* – bread) it sounds like *ow* followed by a slight *oo* (powoo).

Useful words and phrases

hello	**olá**
goodbye	**adeus**
good morning	**bom dia**
good afternoon	**boa tarde**
good evening	**boa noite**
please	**faz favor**
thank you	**obrigada** (F)
	obrigado (M)
yes/no	**sim/não**
do you speak English?	**fala Inglês?**
how are you?	**como está?**
very well	**muito bem**
how much?	**quanta custa?**
very good	**muito bom**
excuse me	**com licença**
sorry/pardon me	**desculpe**
it does not matter	**não faz mal**
good luck	**boa sorte**

In bars/cafés

I would like (a beer)	**queria (cerveja**
please	**faz favor**
Cheers (your health)	**saúde**
enjoy your meal	**bom apetite**
the bill please	**a conta, faz fav**
wine	**vinho**
house wine	**vinho da casa**
white	**branco**
red	**tinto**
rosé	**rosé**
green (young)	**verde**
sparkling	**espumante**
bottle	**garrafa**
half bottle	**meia garrafa**
tea	**chá**
lemon	**limão**
fizzy mineral water	**água com gás**
still mineral water	**água sem gás**
orange juice	**sumo de laranj**
coffee (espresso)	**bica**
coffee (large, strong and black)	**café grande**
coffee (large, weak and black)	**carioca**
coffee with milk (large cup) (literally 'a Chinese lady')	**chinesa**
coffee with milk (small cup)	**garota**
coffee with much milk (tall glass, literally 'a galleon')	**galão**
sugar	**açúcar**

Food

breakfast	**pequeno almoço**
lunch	**almoço**
high tea (meal)	**lanche**
dinner	**jantar**
bread	**pão**
cake	**bolo**
cheese	**queijo**
chicken	**frango**
eggs	**ovos**
fish	**peixe**
fruit	**fruta**
ham	**fiambre**
ice cream	**gelado**
lamb	**borrego**
pork	**porco**
rice	**arroz**
shellfish	**mariscos**
steak	**bife**
tuna	**átum**
veal	**vitela**

Out and about

airport	**aeroporto**
beach	**praia**
bus station	**estação de autocarros**
bus stop	**paragem**
cake shop	**pastelaria**
chemist	**farmácia**
church	**igreja**
danger	**perigo/risco**
doctor	**médico**
market	**mercado**
petrol station	**posto de gasolina**
police station	**posto de policia**
post office	**correios**
supermarket	**supermercado**
swimming pool	**piscina**
telephone	**telefone**
tourist information	**poste de turismo**
toilet	**quarto de banho**
(men/women)	**(senhores/senhoras)**

LOST PROPERTY

There is a good chance that any property you lose (especially if left in a taxi or bus) will be handed in to the lost property office in Funchal: contact Polícia de Perdias & Achados, Rua João de Deus 7 (tel: 222022)

MAPS

Perfectly adequate maps of Funchal and Madeira are given out free by the tourist office, Avenida Arriaga 19, Funchal. For walking, *The Landscapes of Madeira* (4th edition) by John and Pat Underwood is the indispensable guide, with routes plotted on to Portuguese contoured military maps. For driving, the Bartholomew *Madeira Holiday Map* is the most up to date, showing roads that are under construction and due to open in the years ahead. In reading Madeiran maps, it is useful to know the meaning of certain place name elements:

achada	plateau
arco	curving mountain ridge
boca	mouth/mountain pass
cabo	cape
caldeirão	crater or basin
calheta	stream
caminho	path and (confusingly) road
cruzinhas	crossroads
encumeada	summit
fonte	spring
jardim	garden
levada	irrigation canal
lombada	ridge
miradouro	viewpoint
monte	mount
parque	park
praça	square
ribeira	river/river valley
rocha	rock/crag
vale	valley

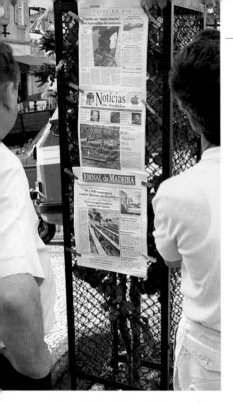

MEDIA

Madeira's main daily newspaper is the *Diário de Notícias*. This produces a four-page English-language supplement which is distributed to most hotels and which summarises local and world news. It also contains a miscellany of information on everything – from the weather, exchange rates and the day's TV and radio schedules, to which cruise liners are in harbour and what is on at the local cinemas and theatre. Supplementing this is the monthly *Madeira Island Bulletin*, free from hotels and the Tourist Office, which contains lots of useful information on restaurants, shops and entertainment. Madeira Tourist Radio (in English) is always worth tuning into if you are in your hotel room at 5.45pm. It broadcasts interesting anecdotes, advice on

pronouncing Portuguese, restaurant recommendations and much more on 96mHz FM daily except Sunday (bear in mind though, that this is a commercial station so that not all of its recommendations are impartial). Most hotels in Funchal have satellite facilities so you can usually pick up 20 or so channels including the American CNN channel for news. A wide range of English newspapers and magazines can be bought in hotel shops or city centre newsagents, usually the day after publication.

MONEY MATTERS

The money used on Madeira is the Portuguese *escudo*, which is divided into 100 *centavos*. The dollar symbol is used in place of a decimal point between the **escudos** and the *centavos*; thus 3$50 means three *escudos* and 50 *centavos*.

Banks and currency exchange

All banks in Funchal offer currency exchange services and their rates are better than those of exchange bureaux or hotels. Banks are open Monday to Friday, 8.30am–3pm, and several of the larger banks, located near the Sé (Cathedral) in Avenida Arriaga, have hole-in-the-wall automatic exchange machines which operate 24 hours a day. Exchange bureaux are open 9am–1pm and 2pm–5pm, Monday to Friday, and 9am–1pm on Saturday. Whether you use a bank or a bureau you must present your passport when changing money, even for cash transactions. It also pays to exchange as much as possible at one go, since there is a standard tax per transaction, no matter how large or small (in 1994 this was 1,000$ to exchange cash and 2,180$ to exchange travellers' cheques).

Cheques and credit cards

Travellers' cheques, Eurocheques and all the major credit cards can be used for obtaining money. Travellers' cheques and Eurocheques may also be used for paying bills in the more up-market, tourist-oriented hotels, shops and restaurants but credit cards are not yet universally accepted.

For small-value transactions and in inexpensive local restaurants, cash is king, and surprisingly even some hotels and restaurants with pretensions to status have yet to join the credit card age.

Value added tax

Value added tax is levied on most luxury goods at rates in excess of 12 per cent. So long as you come from a country outside of the European Union, you can claim a refund of this tax on large purchases. Shops that participate in the Tax Free Shopping scheme; if so, they will have all the necessary forms and will explain how to obtain the refund.

NATIONAL HOLIDAYS

1 January	**New Year's Day**
variable	**Shrove Tuesday**
variable	**Good Friday**
25 April	**Revolution Day**
1 May	**Labour Day**
variable	**Corpus Christi**
10 June	**Camões' Day**
1 July	**Discovery of Madeira Day**
15 August	**Assumption**
21 August	**General Holiday**
5 October	**Republic Day**
1 November	**All Saints' Day Independence**
1 December	**Restoration Day**
8 December	**Immaculate Conception**
25 December	**Christmas Day**
26 December	**St Stephen's Day**

OPENING HOURS

Banks are open Monday to Friday, 8.30am–3pm.

Exchange bureaux (*cambios*) are open Monday to Friday, 9am–1pm and 2pm–5pm; Saturdays 9am–1pm.

Shops are open Monday to Friday, 9am–1pm and 3pm–7pm; Saturday 9am–1pm. These hours are observed strictly by most shops in central Funchal but supermarket chains, such as Lido Sol and Nova Esperanza, are open 10am–9pm/10pm, seven days a week.

PHARMACIES

In Portuguese a chemist or pharmacy is called a *farmácia*. They display a sign consisting of a white cross on a green background and are open Monday to Friday, 9am–1pm and 3pm–7pm; Saturday, 9am–1pm. All pharmacies have a notice on the door showing which chemist is on 24-hour duty that day. English-speaking visitors are catered for at the centrally situated Botica Inglesa, Rua Câmara Pesteria 23–25 (tel: 220158).

PLACES OF WORSHIP

The Madeirans are Roman Catholic and mass is held regularly in churches all around the island.

Madeira has its own Anglican chaplain and services are held at the Church of the Holy Trinity (better known as the English Church – see page 36), Rua do Quebra Costas 18 (tel: 220674), at 11am every Sunday, and refreshments are served afterwards in the well-tended church gardens. The times of other services are posted in hotels and at the Tourist Information Centre, Avenida Arriaga 18.

Baptist services are held in English on Sundays at 6pm at Rua Cidade de

Honolulu 9, while Catholic Mass is said in English at the Igreja da Penha, the church at the back of the Savoy Hotel on Rua do Carvalho Araujo, at 10.30am on Sunday.

POLICE

The fact that the police keep a low profile on Madeira is a tribute to the law-abiding nature of most Madeirans, but the police are there when you need them. Dial 115 in an emergency, otherwise 222022. You can also approach police officers for information or assistance: those wearing a red armband are there to offer help to visitors and speak another language as well as Portuguese – in most cases this means English.

POSTAL SERVICES

Funchal's main post office (*Correios*) is centrally located just up from the statue of Zarco on Avenida Zarco. Most of the staff here speak English. As well as postal transactions, you can also make overseas telephone calls from here, using special

booths which enable you to pay once your call is finished. The post office is open Monday to Friday, 8.30am–8pm, and Saturday 9am–1pm, while the telephone booths stay open until 10pm. In the hotel district there is also a post office in the Lido Sol supermarket complex, Estrada Monumental 318, which is open Monday to Friday, 9am–7pm.

PUBLIC TRANSPORT
Taxis

Madeira's yellow cabs are an easy and cheap way of getting around Funchal. There are ranks at central points in the Hotel Zone, and in the city centre, and you can hail any cab displaying a *livre* (free) sign. Hotels and restaurants will call a cab for you or you can phone for one yourself:
Funchal: 2220911/222000/222500
Machico: 762480

Taxi journeys are metered within Funchal and there are set rates for longer journeys to specific destinations around the island. The official price list should be available for consultation in the taxi; copies are also displayed in the Tourist Information Centre, Avenida Arriaga 18, and on many hotel notice boards.

In theory the rates are also fixed for hiring a cab for the day or half day but in practice you can usually bargain the price down by up to 2,000$. Hiring a taxi by the day means that you can work out your own tour itinerary and if three or four people travel together this is cheaper than renting a self-drive car or joining an organised coach tour. Ask your hotel concierge, tour representative or a travel agent to recommend a driver who speaks English, knows the island well and who drives safely; alternatively ring Central Taxis (tel: 230016). Try to book taxi tours a day or two in advance because good drivers are in demand.

Most taxi drivers are honest (but see page 22); if you feel you have been treated badly you should record the driver's number (displayed on the dashboard and painted on the outside of the front doors); reporting him to the police is a serious matter – simply to threaten to report the driver is probably sufficient to ensure a change of attitude.

Do not, under any circumstances, use unlicensed cabs whose smooth-talking drivers are out to rip you off, either through extortionate fares or by acting as touts for specific shops, restaurants or timeshare developments.

Buses

If you intend to use buses (*autocarros*), be sure you have a lot of time and do not mind close contact with the local people, since they can get crowded. Orange town buses offer a very cheap way of getting around Funchal. The Tourist Office (page 189) has a leaflet giving times and routes. The destination is indicated at the front of the bus. You can pay when you board but it is cheaper to buy tickets in advance in bulk from bus company kiosks on Avenida do Mar – the best deal is a seven-day pass available to visitors only, so you must produce your passport when you buy the ticket.

Long-distance buses can be a useful form of transport for anyone who wants to explore Madeira's *levada* footpaths, since the bus system reaches most parts of the island far more cheaply than taxis. The problem is that the system is very confusing to the ordinary visitor, especially since the recent closure of the old bus terminal at the eastern end of Avenida do Mar. Although this is still marked as the bus station on most maps,

the five main bus companies have, in fact, moved to new stations in different parts of the city. You will find full details of routes and timetables in the daily English supplements to the *Notícias da Madeira* newspaper (distributed free to many hotels) but you will need the following information to work out which bus goes from where:

Country bus stop

SAM buses (cream and green) operating routes 20, 23, 53, 60, 78, 113 and 156 now go from the bus station on Avenida Caloueste Gulbenkian (just up from the roundabout at the western end of Avenida Arriaga).

Rodoeste buses (red, grey and white), operating routes 1, 4, 6, 7, 96, 107, 139, 148 and 154 leave from the Campo da Barca multi-storey car-park on Rua Dr Manuel Pestana Junior (the main road out of Funchal to the airport). The remaining three companies, operating routes 2, 29, 77, 103, 136 and 155, still use the eastern end of Avenida do Mar but are due to move during 1994. Ask your hotel concierge, or enquire at the Tourist Information Centre, Avenida Arriaga 18, for the latest information.

SENIOR CITIZENS

Senior citizens' concessions in Madeira are only available to Portuguese nationals. Several UK-based tour operators specialising in Madeira offer extremely cheap rates on winter-break holidays of three weeks or more (for example, in 1994, the typical cost of a three-month stay was £349 per person, less than £4 per day). Given Madeira's mild winter climate and low cost of living, this can be a very attractive alternative to spending winter in chilly northern Europe.

STUDENT/YOUTH TRAVEL

If you are visiting Madeira on a budget, go for lower-cost flights via Lisbon rather than the more expensive direct flights, travel by bus, and shop for food in local markets. Cheap accommodation can be had in *pensãos* (pensions) in most villages, though Funchal is geared to the up-market traveller and has little in the way of budget accommodation. Some visitors to Madeira dispense with accommodation and either camp (see Camping, page 177) or sleep under the stars, using an all-weather sleeping bag. In the dry months of July and August this is perfectly possible and the views of the night sky can be superb.

TELEPHONES

Local calls are easily made from coin-operated phones which take 10, 20 and 50 *escudos* coins. For international calls it is cheapest to buy a card from post offices and shops displaying the Credifone symbol and use the card phones that can be found all over Funchal. Alternatively, you can use the metered telephone booths at the main post office (see Postal Services, page 186) and pay at the end of your call. You

can, of course dial direct from your hotel room, but you will pay a hefty premium for the convenience.

To call another European country dial 00 followed by the country code (Ireland 353, UK 44, then the area code, omitting the initial 0, then the subscriber number).

To call outside Europe, dial 097 followed by the country code (USA and Canada 1, Australia 61, New Zealand 64, South Africa 27).

Directory enquiries (Madeira): 118
Operator: 090
International operator: 099

TIME

Madeira observes Greenwich Mean Time (GMT) in winter (end of September to end of March) and GMT plus 1 hour in summer. Thus in summer, Madeira is 5 hours ahead of Eastern Standard Time, 8 hours ahead of Pacific Time, 1 hour behind Lisbon and much of Europe, 2 hours behind South Africa, 9 behind Australia and 12 behind New Zealand.

TIPPING

On Madeira, nobody demands tips as a right or treats you differently if you do not tip – indeed, people seem pleasantly surprised when a tip is offered. So as not to spoil that situation it is best to reserve your tips for people who give you exceptionally good service, rather than tipping people just for doing their job – in any event, most hotel and restaurant bills already include a service charge.

TOILETS

Hotels, bars, restaurants and museums have toilets for public use and these are usually modern and clean. Doors are usually marked *senhoras* (women) and *senhores* (men); fortunately for those who cannot remember which is which, they usually carry some kind of identifying symbol as well.

TOURIST INFORMATION

Funchal's Tourist Information Office is centrally located at Avenida Arriaga 18 and is open Monday to Friday, 9am–8pm; Saturday, 9am–6pm. The English-speaking staff are genuinely helpful and will supply free maps as well as answers to just about any question you may have. You can telephone as well (tel: 225658) but the office is really geared to the needs of people who visit in person. Within the office there is also a currency exchange bureau and a booking desk where you can sign up for organised tours. There are smaller offices, with more restricted opening hours, in the arrivals lounge of Santa Catarina airport, and in Machico, at the Edifício Paz, Rua do Ribeirinho (tel: 965712).

Tourist Offices Overseas

For information on Madeira before you leave home, there are Portuguese National Tourist Offices in many cities around the world, including:
Canada: 60 Bloor St West, Suite 1005, Toronto, Ontario M4W 3B8 (tel: 416–921 7376).
UK: 22–25A Sackville St, London W1X 1DE (tel: 071 494 1441).
USA: 590 Fifth Avenue, 4th Floor, New York, NY 10036–4704).

TRAVEL AGENTS

There are numerous travel agents in the Hotel Zone and in central Funchal and they will help you choose the coach excursions, boat trips, *levada* walking tours or jeep safaris that are best for you. Among leading agents and operators are:

Blandys, Avenida das Comunidades Madeirenses 1 (tel: 220161/232065) – everything from round-the-island tours to folk evenings or mini cruises.
Madeira Express, Avenida Arriaga 38–40 (tel: 225250) – besides daily minibus tours of the island, with tape-recorded commentaries, this company will also put together tailor-made tours and provide fully qualified private guides.
Sociedade de Animação Turistica, Sítio da Igreja, 9135 Camacha (tel: 922288). A small company specialising in guided *levada* walks and mountain-bike tours.
Madeira Safari, Rua António José de Almeida (tel: 228684). Off-road adventure tours along the mountain tracks used by forest and national park wardens.

Inspired by the local colours

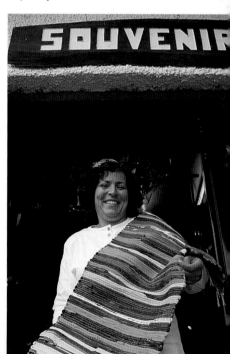

ACKNOWLEDGEMENTS

The Automobile Association wishes to thank the following organisations, libraries and photographers for their assistance in the preparation of this book.

MARY EVANS PICTURE LIBRARY 13b
CHRISTOPHER HILL PHOTOGRAPHIC 5, 14, 81, 154/5, 175
NATURE PHOTOGRAPHERS LTD 134 (P R Sterry), 135 (D A Smith)
PORTO SANTO DIVING CENTRE 134/5
SPECTRUM COLOUR LIBRARY cover
THE MANSELL COLLECTION 34a, 35.

The remaining pictures are held in the AA Photo Library and were taken by Jon Wyand with the exception of Inset, Spine and pages 17, 18, 20, 22, 26, 28, 29, 46, 46/7, 47b, 82b, 83, 102, 107a, 116a, 130, 138a, 150a, 150/1, 151, 153, 159, 166 and 167b, which were taken by Peter Baker, and page 157a which was taken by Wyn Voysey.

The Automobile Association would also like to thank João Cardeira of Automóvel Club de Portugal and Mrs Pilar Pereira of the Portuguese Tourist Organisation for their help in the preparation of this book.

CONTRIBUTORS
Series adviser: Melissa Shales **Designer:** Design 23 **Copy editor:** Dilys Jones
Verifier: Joanna Whitaker **Indexer:** Marie Lorimer